Journal of Visua

The *Journal of Visual A*
National Association
will publish scholarly
art seen from an edu
scholars, art educator
positions and practic
practice and educatic

The *Journal of Vis*
of interpretive and ed
particularly those whi
contexts. Accepting tl
the journal will not re
or methodology. It wi
separate section, mor
understanding and de
relationship to relatec
technologies.

The *Journal of Vis*
National Association

Editorial Board

Editorial Assistant

Sophie Pagett
Faculty of Art, Media and Design
University of the West of England
Bower Ashton Campus
Clanage Rd
Bristol BS3 2JT
UK.
e-mail: <Sophie.Pagett@uwe.ac.uk>

The *Journal of Visual Art Practice* is published three times per year by Intellect, PO
Box 862, Bristol BS99 1DE, UK. The current subscription rates are £30 (personal)
and £75 (institutional). A postage charge of £8 is made for subscriptions outside
of Europe. Enquiries and bookings for advertising should be addressed to the
Journals Manager at Intellect.

ISSN 1470-2029

Printed and bound in Great Britain by
the Cromwell Press, Wiltshire

Contributions

Opinion

The views expressed in the *Journal of Visual Art Practice* are those of the authors, and do not necessarily coincide with those of the Editor or the Editorial Advisory Board.

Referees

Journal of Visual Art Practice is a refereed journal. Referees are chosen for their expertise within the subject area. They are asked to comment on comprehensibility, originality and scholarly worth of the article submitted.

Length

Articles should not normally exceed 6000 words in length.

Submitting

Articles should be original and not be under consideration by any other publication.

In the first instance, contributions should be submitted in hard copy only. Three hard copies must be sent to the Editor, typewritten or printed on one side only, and double-spaced.

If the article is accepted, it should be put on disk, with any required amendments, and this electronic version of the article as agreed for final publication should then be sent to the Editor. The electronic version should be in WORD, and be submitted along with an ASCII (i.e. Text-only) file of the article on a 3.5 inch disk, along with a hard-copy version. The disk should be labelled with the name of the author, the title of the article, and the software used. (Formats other than WORD are not encouraged, but please contact the Editor for further details.)

Language

The journal uses standard British English. The Editor reserves the right to alter usage to this end. Because of the interdisciplinary nature of the readership, jargon should be kept to a minimum.

Format

The journal is set with Apple Macintosh equipment and reset using Quark; it is therefore best if the use of automatic footnoting devices is avoided.

Illustrations

Illustrations are welcome. In particular, discussions of particular buildings, sites or landscapes would be assisted by including illustrations.

Generally only black and white is available. Photographs should be black and white glossy. All slides should be printed as colour photos or copied onto PhotoCD as a YCC computer file.

Line drawings, maps, diagrams etc. should be in a camera-ready state, capable of reduction, or as Macintosh EPS or TIFF files with hard copy output.

All illustrations, photographs, diagrams, maps etc. should follow the same numerical sequence and be shown as Figure 1, Figure 2 etc.

The source has to be indicated beneath the text. Copyright clearance should be indicated by the contributor and is always the responsibility of the contributor. When they are on a separate sheet or file, indication must be given as to where they should be placed in the text.

Quotations

Paragraph quotations must be indented with an additional one line space above and below and without quotes.

Captions

All illustrations should be accompanied by a caption, which should include the Fig. No., and an acknowledgement to the holder of the copyright. **The author has responsibility to ensure that the proper permissions are obtained.**

Other Styles

Margins should be at least one inch all round and pagination should be continuous. Foreign words and phrases inserted in the text should be italicized.

Author note

A note on each author is required and this should include an institution or address. This should not exceed 50 words. Authors should also indicate how they wish their names to appear. The custom is without titles, one forename plus surname, but authors may vary this. The author should also provide a short sentence (of no more than sixteen words) stating their name and institutional affiliation or their identification (to appear at the bottom of page one of their contribution).

Abstract

Each article should be accompanied by an abstract, which should not exceed 150 words in length and should concentrate on the significant findings.

Notes

Notes will appear at the side of appropriate pages, but the numerical sequence runs throughout the article. These should be kept as short as possible and to a minimum, be identified by a superscript numeral. Please avoid the use of automatic footnoting programmes; simply append the footnotes to the end of the article.

References and Bibliography

Bibliographical references within the notes must adhere to the following models:

Books: author's full name, title (italics), place of publication, publisher, year, and page reference.

Articles: author's full name, title (within single quotation marks), name of journal (italics), volume and issue numbers, date, and page reference.

A bibliography may be included if this is deemed to be a necessary addition to the sidenotes.

Reviewing

Please contact the Editor if you are interested in reviewing for this journal.

The Editor welcomes contributions. Any matters concerning the format and presentation of articles not covered by the above notes should be addressed to the Editor.

Contributors

Katy Macleod is a Senior Lecturer in Art History at the University of Plymouth. She coordinates the Critical Studies programme for the BA Fine Art course. She has been actively researching into and writing about the creative practice higher degree culture since 1996.

Lin Holdridge is a Researcher in the Faculty of Arts and Education at the University of Plymouth. She has been researching with Katy Macleod in the field of creative practice higher research degrees since 1998 and they have published several collaborative papers, both in the UK and Europe.

Ken Neil is Head of Fine Art at Gray's School of Art in Aberdeen. He studied art history and painting at Edinburgh University and Edinburgh College of Art. He has recently completed a PhD that considered the significance of the 'banal' reproduction of the everyday in the painting of the American photorealists.

Malcolm Miles is Reader in Cultural Theory at the University of Plymouth, and contributes to the MA Architecture and Cultural Studies at Oxford Brookes University. He is author of *Art, Space & The City* (Routledge, 1997) and *The Uses of Decoration: Essays in the Architectural Everyday* (Wiley, 2000), and co-editor of (forthcoming) *Urban Futures* (Routledge, 2003).

Naren Barfield, Senior Lecturer and MA Artist-Teacher Coordinator. Wimbledon School of Art, Merton Hall Road, London SW19 3QA Tel: 020 8408 5042/3. Fax: 020 8408 5050. E-mail: nbarfield@wimbledon.ac.uk

RyyA. Bread© has recently completed a PhD in critical art practice methodology at Falmouth College of Arts, Cornwall.

Clive Cazeaux is Senior Lecturer in Aesthetics at the University of Wales Institute, Cardiff. He is the editor of *The Continental Aesthetics Reader* (Routledge, 2000), and the author of articles on metaphor, art theory and practice, and modern European philosophy.

Jim Mooney is an artist and writer who is Tutor in Painting at the RCA and Reader in the Theory and Practice of Fine Art at Middlesex University. He completed his Ph.D. in 1999, entitled *Praxis-Ethics-Erotics*. He exhibits regularly in Britain and abroad.

Karen Wallis is a practising artist and Visiting Lecturer at the University of the West of England, Bristol. Her recently completed PhD, here presented as work in progress, is entitled *PAINTING & DRAWING THE NUDE: a search for a realism for the body through phenomenology & fine art practice.*

Partou Zia was born in Tehran, Persia (now Iran). Partou is an award-winning artist living and working in Newlyn, Cornwall. A graduate of Warwick University [BA History of Art], and Slade School of Art, UCL [BA Painting], she completed her Ph.D. at FCA and Plymouth University in September 2001.

Deborah Robinson is an artist whose work explores liquidity and light in relation to the body through painting and alternative darkroom processes. She has taught painting and theory at universities in Britain and Los Angeles and is at present a part-time lecturer in Fine Art at the University of Plymouth.

Trish Lyons is a Senior Lecturer in Sculpture at Camberwell College of Art, London. She completed her PhD on the mimetic in Fine Art practice at Central Saint Martins, London Institute and has exhibited widely. She is currently investigating the potential applications of biomimetics in Art and Design practice.

Kenneth Hay is a practising artist. He is Senior Lecturer in Fine Art at the University of Leeds, where he has established the higher-degree culture. His work is widely exhibited and published.

Elizabeth Price exhibits regularly as an artist. She completed her PhD in Fine Art at the University of Leeds in 2001. She now teaches at Goldsmiths College, University of London.

Editorial

Iain Biggs

This double issue, the first of its kind produced by JVAP, is particularly timely. It builds on an ongoing investigation by Katy Macleod and Lin Holdridge, our guest editors, into the nature of creative practice research degrees. (In the past Katy has contributed articles to *Drawing Fire* vol. 2 nos. 2, 3 and 4 on related topics, which have also been the focus of very valuable conferences at the University of Plymouth). As this issue of JVAP goes to the publisher, Katy Macleod and Lin Holdridge will be acting as co-ordinators for one of the ten symposia organized as part of the 2002 ELIA Conference, Dublin. Together with Siún Hanrahan and Sally Jane Norman, Katy and Lin will be facilitating debate between academics drawn from across the European League of Institutes for the Arts, under the heading 'Monstrous Thinking: on Practice-based Research'. I am, in consequence, particularly grateful to them for making time to guest-edit this double issue.

The tensions and opportunities surrounding creative practice research degrees are, of course, profoundly important in their own right. The guest editors make it very clear why we have devoted a double issue to this area of work. However, the issues involved also provide one of the rare sites in higher education where it is still possible to detect open manifestations of an ancient cultural fear. It is clear that the university system has yet to come fully to terms with its instinctive iconophobia; an iconophobia inherited from its Judaeo-Christian past, particularly in its Protestant manifestation, and perpetuated by the Enlightenment's pursuit of 'radical monotheism' by other, secular, means. Manifestations of this deep-seated psychological fear, together with its implications for the larger cultural context, add another, not inconsequential, level of interest to debates around creative practice research and the academy's 'disciplining' of practice-based pedagogy.

JVAP 2 (1&2) 4 ©Intellect Ltd 2002

The Enactment of Thinking:
creative practice research degrees

Katy Macleod and Lin Holdridge

Abstract

This editorial serves to introduce the papers from the conference 'The Enactment of Thinking: creative practice research degrees', University of Plymouth (2001). It examines several critical debates arising from the conference, and in particular, highlights the two central themes which were consistently addressed: the material positioning of the artist (i.e. subjecthood) and ontological speculation about 'being in the world'. We cite examples of these themes through doctoral papers dealing with the question of research methodology; ontological and subjective spatial research paradigms and mimesis in practice. We give philosophical precedence to the phenomenological and ontological speculations of artist/researchers through the work of Merleau-Ponty whose work not only brings philosophy much closer to art, but also provides a specific framework which both enlivens and validates the material and ontological positioning of the artist/researcher. The paper responds to our research which defines an understanding of visual intellectuality, its rigour and integrity, within this doctoral field.

The conference was designed to advance nationally-based research into the complex intellectuality of creative practice and to acknowledge its potential contribution to the broader research culture.

'The Enactment of Thinking: creative practice research degrees', University of Plymouth (2001), was a sequel conference to 'The Relationship of Making to Writing: practice, history, theory', University of Plymouth (1998). Both conferences built on research in the field of practice-led research (Frayling 1993; Seago 1994; Newbury 1996; Hockey 1999; Macleod 2000 et al.). Research to date has been very much involved with exploring the nature of this new research field; particularly the issue of appropriate methodologies. 'The Enactment of Thinking' focused upon and revealed the rigour and integrity of visual intellectuality. Conference speakers were drawn from a range of disciplines, including the host discipline of Fine Art: Philosophy, Music, Performance Arts, Film and Art History. The programme was devised not just to showcase impressive research undertaken in the fulfilment of a creative practice research degree, but also to broaden the debate and to extend thinking beyond the confines of a single discipline to reflect more accurately the interdisciplinarity and intertextuality of research by art practice.

Critical debate arising from the conference examined, amongst other ideas; the material positioning of the artist-thinker as subject; the four-dimensionality of the space for visual thinking; thinking outside the categories for mental and physical action using metaphor; and, most insistently, on states of being precipitated by practice. It was clear that ontological speculation about being in the world is at the heart of creative practice research. The question of the material positioning of the artist as the subject of his/her own enquiry, as well as subject to semiotic systems of social signification, was the central question being addressed throughout the

1 This paper was made available to delegates at the time of the conference. However, it is now being exclusively published by Middlesex University.

conference. This remained the case, regardless of whether the individual practice was involved in idealistic, socially transformative actions or investigating the complexity of spatial investigation through the use of computer technologies. It was this ontological speculation which removed debate from the much narrower confines previously established in the research culture (Hockey 1999; Macleod 2000), where research findings had led to anxious discussion about the subjective identification of the artist/researcher expressed as a resistance to objective and social accountability. 'The Enactment of Thinking' registered a much more provocative understanding of the subjecthood of artist/researchers who are engaged in negotiating vulnerable and oscillating subjecthoods, where states of being are necessarily critically engaged with the condition of being. In this sense, the conference marks an important advance in the thinking that serves to contextualize creative practice research. In identifying the particular condition of subjecthoods which are socially and critically engaged, we can now properly conceive of enacted thinking as having the potential to be both academically and culturally transformative.

Creative practice research takes us to the edge of dialectical reason. It removes itself from the outdated insistence on a separation of theory from practice, of making from writing, and instead seeks to use the tension between linguistic and rhetorical modes.

Since 1998 debate has shifted towards closer consideration of the intellectuality and the propositional reasoning of visual thinking, and so to examining the complex issue of 'methodology' or, rather, the nature of the methodology which underpins a creative practice research submission. It is, of course, axiomatic to assert that research methodology demonstrates the research premise on which the research is predicated. Previously, however, literature in the field has overemphasized the importance of methodology (Gray 1995; Gray and Pirie 1995). Recent research by artists has redefined the literature in this respect. Jim Mooney has, for example, provided an exemplary discourse on *Research in Fine Art by Project: General Remarks Toward Definition and Legitimation of Methodologies.*[1]

Here Mooney cites:

> ... The invariable fact is that a piece of work which ceaselessly proclaims its determination for method is ultimately sterile ... the researcher repeatedly asserts that his text will be methodological but the text never comes. No surer way to kill a piece of research and send it to join the great waste of abandoned projects than Method. (Barthes 1977: 201)

Mooney's intention was not to refuse method or the importance of a sound research methodology. Rather, he demonstrated that the teleological nature of methodologies advanced as appropriate to the artist/researcher are inappropriate as conceptual schemas because they do not take account of the a posteriori nature of art knowledge. Mooney's original doctoral research results in the advocacy of a rhizomatic model (Deleuze and Guatttari 1988: 25) involving connections between semiotic chains of signification.

The work of art is a site of gathering and ordering (re-articulation) of the gatherings, producing new matrices, new bodies, new conjunctions of semiotic chains.

Katy Macleod and Lin Holdridge

Mooney has developed an original line of argument about the semiotic functioning of artworks, to underpin his proposition that art practice is not teleologically inscribed nor is it subject to extant 'theory'. Through the 'Enactment of Thinking' it is possible to advocate a new understanding of the relation between theory and art practice research. It is possible to assert that advanced art practice research is *necessarily* theorized practice.

It is the methodology that determines the quality of the artist's theoretical premise and this resides in the artwork. Nevertheless, the visual *enactment of thinking* will only be revealed and understood at the moment of the Viva, when the examiner/viewer interacts with the *alatheic* quality and power of the artist/researcher's visual thinking. This is 'live time' - the outcome cannot be predetermined or prejudged. However, this live time element creates a tension and a resistance throughout the doctoral research (by its very nature), and is a constant characteristic of the process. It therefore refuses a priori knowledge; the revealing of knowledge is always a posteriori. It uses neither traditional academic nor diachronic reasoning, because the process of work is always synchronically embodied in current culture. Live time is both crucial and radical in its refusal of the conventional academic doctorate. It holds an intellectual persuasiveness that is constituted by the tension created between the normative academic culture and the broader culture of the life world. It refuses predictive methodologies, it is neither fixed in advance, nor critically engaged; rather it operates in a fluid, paradoxical, almost Bergsonian space. Above all, live time is inextricably linked to an ontological base: the artist/researcher is engaging in a process of philosophical subjecthood within a phenomenological discourse.

Subjectivity and the artists have long been bedfellows. The 'subjectivity' of the artist as opposed to the 'objectivity' of the scientist is a familiar and well-trodden path of misnomers. This positioning of the artist as subjective/self-reflexive, indeed, self-indulgent, has perpetrated and perpetuated the myth of the artist as a 'non-academic'. However, with the artist/researcher and the culture of creative practice doctoral research now firmly in place, such misconceptions need to be swept aside. Earlier research into the culture revealed that the subjective identification of the artist/researcher was expressed as an insistence on social privacy. However the 'Enactment of Thinking' generated debate which focused intensely upon the subject of subjecthood itself.

Naren Barfield, in his doctoral submission *Integrated Artworks: Theory and Practice in Relation to Printmaking and Computers, and the influence of 'non-Euclidean geometry' and the 'fourth dimension' on developments in Twentieth-Century Pictorial Space*, produced an analysis of a research methodology precisely concomitant with what we have outlined above. His research dealt with spatial ontology, digital print and the 'fourth dimension' of space. His paper indicated that the research submission was a highly intertextual development of spatially orientated fine art practice. Such practice adapted and integrated methods, examining relations between spatial art theory and practice, digital technology, print and photomechanical imaging methods, hyperspace philosophy and twentieth-century art historical analysis of developments in pictorial space. He created original artworks which carry imagery whilst making interventions into physical space and which embody theoretical knowledge within the physical artefact.

These interventions are both ontological and subjective and as such, the viewer becomes aware, whilst studying the imagery, of the sense of 'live time' - that moment of understanding which is indeed revealed by the artwork. This methodology borrows from a wide, diverse and interdisciplinary range of subjects. As the artist/researcher incorporated these sources into his practice, the practice, subsuming them, became the methodology that drove the doctoral submission. The submission was a research into knowledge, but the art practice research dictated the terms of the ongoing research and as such, the submission constituted new knowledge in itself.

Creative practice research exacts a strong levy on existing theory, and involves an intellectual process which is unconventional and, perhaps, unacceptable to the broader cultures of higher degree research. For instance, in Trish Lyons' research submission *Mimesis in Practice*, the foundational theory for mimesis was clearly identified as Plato's. However, this doctoral research did not seek to exemplify Plato's theory of mimesis, it sought to reveal mimesis in *action through practice*. The research process involved making moulds and casts from the artist's body, alginate moulds and bronze casts. It was an intensive highly complex set of research processes, each part of which was documented. We will contend that it was not until the visual documentation was made and viewed that *mimesis in art practice* was revealed. In other words it was not until the visual documentation of mimesis that the theoretical proposition was revealed, and, when it was revealed, it demonstrated a set of complex relations between artist, mould and cast - a set of interchangeable subject/object relations quite distinct from Plato's theory of mimesis. However, rather than rule out Plato's theory, it adds further charges of more recent theory about constructed and constructing selves following Foucault and Lacan in particular and, most important for our purposes, offers a visual/intellectual speculation about *being in the world* and about the presence of the artist/author in relation to art and representation.

Mimesis in Practice provides some indication of what we take to be the theorization of practice. Most interestingly, for our purposes, this doctoral submission provides little evidence in words of what has been formulated by the research art practice. This thesis (written texts and artworks) offers ambiguous art knowledge. It is difficult for us to accept ambiguity as valid within the context of higher degree research, where clarity of research intentions and, ultimately, the 'communication of new knowledge' are of paramount importance. However, ambiguity has been readily accepted by Mooney in *Research in Fine Art by Project* as entirely appropriate to art practice research, where there is, as Eagleton asserts for poetry, an *internal communication*: a poem can only be re-read because its *condensed systems of communication contain tensions, parallelisms, repetitions and oppositions* which continually modify each other. This appears to be an exact description of the imaged relationships of artist to mould and to cast, a dense and complex matrixial theoretical construction which revisits Plato's theory of mimesis, the artist's own working of the concept, the unpremeditated interaction of idea and material and the subject and object of representation. It is this that we take to be the theorization *within* a sculptural practice. It does involve *tensions, parallelism, repetitions and oppositions* that do *modify each other*, determining that this theory *is* ambiguous.

We may not yet be satisfied that this research into mimesis in practice presents theory which is communicable. This is a problem that has been frequently approached and most notably articulated through the policies and papers of the

Katy Macleod and Lin Holdridge

CNAA and the UKCGE. It is, in our view, a problem which will not be resolved until we have learnt more fully to understand the intellectuality of art practice. This is one supervisor/examiner's articulation of the problem:

> We still keep on falling into that position where there is practice and there is theory ... there is a thesis constructed of texts and objects but the texts and objects may, in fact, have been generated by the practice, so that in the end, the thesis is simply practice. Then the difficulty one's got is, if in the end *someone comes along when all the ideas and thinking are embodied in a particular object ... the dilemma there is not that the process can't be used as a submission, the question there is whether we have the skills to read it. It is not the problem of the generation of it, it is the problem of reading it.* (Macleod 1997)

In each of the doctoral examples given, the research methodology has been instrumental to the *visual demonstration* of research findings. Here research knowledge is embedded in ontological speculation about the artist's own material presence in the research project, her/his consciousness is enacted, objectified, cast into art to be re-read by the viewer/examiner.

The phenomenological and ontological speculations of the artist/researcher, as evinced by the conference speakers, have a philosophical precedence, most particularly in the work of Merleau-Ponty. His views on language, perception, ambiguity and the importance of the body, bring philosophy much closer to art. They therefore warrant closer examination as potentially providing a useful framework that can both enlighten and validate the material positioning of the artist-thinker as subject and her/his ontological speculations about *being in the world*. Merleau-Ponty's work precedes structuralism, but his development of the concept of human subjectivity as ambiguous, and his increased emphasis on the study of language, anticipate both the decentring of the subject in structural and post-structural thought and the linguistic emphasis of subsequent French philosophy.

For Merleau-Ponty, true philosophical knowledge is perception. The aim of phenomenology is the direct understanding of reality:

> it is pure and, one might say, non-formalised experience which must be made to achieve the pure expression of its own meaning (Merleau-Ponty 1962: 254).

According to Merleau-Ponty, we are haunted by the pre-reflective world from which we have emerged and our relations with it are therefore pre-conscious, pre-scientific and pre-objective. They are a direct perceptive awareness of our relationship with it. The world can be seen as an *immense individual*; a kind of essential force which informs time or existence, and results in a ceaseless creation of beings or subjectivities. *We are the emergence of time.* Merleau-Ponty refers back to the Kantian notion of time making itself through man:

> The world is inseparable from the subject which is nothing but project (sic) of the world, and the subject is inseparable from the world, but from a world which it projects. The subject, the *I*, fashions the reality of the world through language, and the relationship of the *I* to the world is a constantly modifying synthesis moving towards its conclusion which is to identify itself as an

affirmation of the existence of an ontological reality or Being. (Merleau-Ponty 1962: 491)

Merleau-Ponty refutes Descartes *cogito* however. He says that *cogito* presumes pre-reflective contact of oneself with oneself as what he calls *tacit cogito*, which is impossible:

> It is not the *I think* which pre-eminently contains the *I am*, it is not my existence which is reduced to the consciousness I have of it; it is, on the contrary, the *I think* which is reintegrated into the movement of transcendence of the *I am*, and consciousness into existence.
> 'In order to be aware of the idea of thinking ... to return to immanence and to the consciousness of ... it is necessary to have words. (Merleau-Ponty 1962: 439)

Words are the necessary bridge to construct this transcendental consciousness which emerges from the prevailing creative silence of the pre-reflective world. The philosopher, like the artist, thus passes from semi-obscure darkness to light and knowledge: there is a being of language that repeats the being of Being so that to think is to pass from the source of being to speech or existence. Merleau-Ponty's 'Le Visible et l'Invisible sums up his philosophical aim:

> ... the whole of philosophy consists in recreating a power of signifying, a dawning of meaning, or an uncharted meaning, an expression of experience through experience which illuminates the special domain of language. And in a sense, as Valery says, language is all, since it is nobody's voice; it is the true voice of things, waters and woods. (Merleau-Ponty 1969: 203-04)

The philosophical possibilities of scrutinizing Being are most effective when language is used creatively, as it is used in art:

> The words most laden with philosophy are not necessarily those which enclose what they say. They are those which open most energetically upon being, because they convey more exactly the life of the whole and disturb to breaking point, our well-established certainties. The question is whether philosophy as a rediscovery of unfathomed being can best be served by means of logical language or by using language not as a means of conveying direct, immediate meaning, but as an equivalent of what it would like to say. (Merleau-Ponty 1969: 358)

Language, as a creative instrument rather than a means of communication, is invested with a certain autonomy, an ability to capture or unveil *a meaning which until then had never been objectified;* and this unveiling concerns Being. It is an entry into the Mallarméan world in which language can suggest musically, the presence of absence. It is this presence of absence for which the artist/researcher needs:

> to find a language that could enable things to speak ... what matters is not the actual meaning of each word and each image, but the cognate relationships and connections which are implied in their movement and exchanges. This is also

Katy Macleod and Lin Holdridge

the language of poetry, the language of the imagination which does not describe and define, but which unveils the truth or being of things ... Being is what requires form in creation so that we may experience it. (Merleau-Ponty 1969: 167)

2 Kenneth G. Hay, 'Concrete abstractions - a Della Volpean perspective on studio practice as research' (See this issue).

Merleau-Ponty regards the arts as vehicles for the unveiling of truths; their intrinsic value is to demonstrate that beyond sound, light or coherences in words, there are elements waiting to emerge into visibility, sound and meaning. The body is neither ideation nor object; it is both, and therefore the measure of that which surrounds it:

If one explained completely the architectonics of the human body, its ontological structure and the way it sees and hears itself, one would see that the structure of its silent world is such that all possibilities of speech are already contained in it. (Merleau-Ponty 1969: 203)

The artist's immanent function is to go beyond what one can see, in Merleau-Ponty's terms, as the unformulated truth; to express or reveal what it is to be in the world, to make it cognizant to the senses and to the imagination, to make the invisible visible. It is this which mirrors the phenomenological and ontological concerns of the artist/researcher.

One sign of an active research culture is that curious people continue to seek after specific knowledges, building upon previous conceptions and methodologies to better understand 'what it is to be in the world'. It is a sign of life.[2]

...While I am thinking I am just over here...

Ken Neil

Abstract

This essay is intended as a provocative dramatization of the researcher by creative practice 'becoming aware' of his/her agency in the process of inquiry. It maintains that the agency of the researcher who employs the methods of creative practice is of central importance to the efficacy of the outputs and not something which needs to be suppressed. The question raised implicitly might be this: 'How do we recuperate this agency into our reflection on the outcome of research by creative practice for the purposes of critical evaluation (RAE) and, of course, assessment (Degree Awards)?' The spatial model within the essay proposes that the researcher by creative practice inhabits a productive 'enacting limbo' between the objects of inquiry and the critical reflection on that inquiry. This limbo is rendered productive when the creative researcher somehow sees their being within the structures of the research.

Preamble

This essay needs some explanation. Rather than have the paper address general issues arising from the theme of research by creative practice, the idea for the conference was to present a keynote in direct response to the given theme of the symposium i.e. 'The Enactment of Thinking'. The intention then was for the attendees to bear witness to 'the thinking behind the paper being enacted through its delivery'. At risk of a tautological collapse, for the presentation at times seemed to beg its own questions, the paper attempted to reveal the agency of the creative thinker in the act of creative thinking. The *location* of this agency in relation to

1) the inquiry into the work
2) the final work; and
3) the viewer, is the underlying theme of this re-presentation.

A subtext (one which collides with the operations of the RAE and with post-structuralist recommendations vis-à-vis authorship) is that this agency will not disappear from research by creative practice.

  This points to the genesis of the investigation: the fact that the agency of the 'artist' is both a boon and a disadvantage to the process of research by creative practice. This agency can be a seductive decoy. It can, as noted, lead to an investigative tautology which would see the researcher by creative practice bedazzled by their own reflection. On the other hand, it can lead the creative practitioner to substantive and previously unseen research discoveries. The creative agency of the inquirer can generate novel lines of thought and conclusion which might not emerge otherwise in, as I term it below, a 'mainline narrative.' Such a mainline narrative of inquiry, I imply, is directed by normative strategies of analysis, even if these are current and advanced theoretical devices. New art history, for example, has tutored us to acknowledge the sociocultural drivers behind the authoring of any work, but attending to these drivers is not quite the same as the creative practitioner attending to him/her*self* and the effects of their own agency. If the researcher by creative practice can *locate* themselves in the process of inquiry and somehow sustain a parenthetical reflection on that 'location' (a reflection which is also necessary to the location in the first place), then perhaps the advantages of the presence of the creative agent will prevail. For, to my mind, no other form of academic inquiry can claim quite the same degree of critical immanence and *becoming*.

At the conference, in the attempt to figuratively locate the agency of the creative inquirer, an allusion was drawn to the theatrical soliloquy: an aside to the audience, in parenthesis, which critically informs the mainline narrative of the play but which can also, within the syntax of the drama, appear to be a 'speech to the self'. The sketch which follows here is structured with this model in mind, although it lacks the literal, spatial positioning enacted on the day of the conference. The model is immediately imperfect. This recognition is in part the conclusion of the essay, for the agency of the creative practice researcher cannot separate itself from itself as easily as the model suggests. That conundrum moves this, in fact, *any* discussion of 'agency' towards an Existentialist figuring of the active self - a theme which, with hindsight, preoccupied the conference. In short, creative practice research by dint of the agency of the inquirer is founded on a fascinating simultaneity of presence, self-awareness of presence and the impact of that awareness on the objects of inquiry.

The sketch below begins with a 'voice' from the mainline narrative of the play, so to speak, and moves between that location and somewhere on the 'apron' of the page - the position of the soliloquy. Most of the 'play' takes place as an aside to the reader and to the soliloquizer himself. At the finish the script returns to the 'surface', to the mainline narrative - perhaps a starting point for subsequent essays. To what end? Well, in attempting to locate 'agency' within the process of research by creative practice, the essay sets out to demonstrate that that agency and its recognition by the agent of inquiry ultimately results in the researcher by creative practice being 'positioned between' the two 'points on the stage' - in a 'productive limbo.' This limbo requires a perhaps imperceptible oscillation between the two positions, hence my use of 'simultaneity' above. In turn, this productive limbo generates an awareness in the viewer that the creative agent has both *e*ffected and *a*ffected themselves and their objects of inquiry in the process of research by creative practice - leaving a body of work which illuminates itself precisely because of the presence of a critical and creative agent and not *despite* that presence. A lingering question might be: 'How can we recuperate this agency into our reflection on the outcome of research by creative practice for the purposes of critical evaluation (RAE) and, of course, assessment (Degree Awards)?'

Lastly, apologies, because the dramatization here is not 'costumed'; there is no 'dressing' of the structures being analysed. That I will leave to other papers herein which address specific outputs of research by creative practice. In what follows there is no one specific issue being played out other than the important one of *being* played out.

* *I am about to declaim and denote ...*

... but before I do - here are some thoughts in parenthesis. In some ways, this writing up of a paper delivered six months ago requires something of the process of

...While I am thinking I am just over here...

'enacted thinking' which I addressed at the conference. Logically, it requires me to re-enact the event and replay the critical intentions of the paper whilst being cognizant of the context having changed. The writing up requires me to somehow resuscitate my own thoughts, to bring to life something which was my own, something which is now less 'present participle' than 'past'. My present delivery, which from *here*, this parenthetical position, is cogitating and musing, is dependent on me somehow *seeing me being me* in the event past. For this essay to work, as a readable parenthesis in its own right and as an analogy of sorts, I will need to critically recuperate a *critical self* in the present.

From *this* position at least, a relationship forms between myself now and myself then: I am both *with-in this text* and *with-out this text*. It was intended then, and is intended now, to evoke a sense of the positioning of the creative thinker in the act of creative thinking; a sense of the possible simultaneity of the 'mainline narrative' (the chosen field of inquiry) and the 'self-aware critical reflection' on a) that mainline narrative *per se*, and b) the presence of the creative self in that inquiry into the mainline narrative. The suggestion in this soliloquy is that the *agency* of the creative inquirer, the creative practice researcher, might be located in a parenthetical state in relation to the tier of the mainline narrative of the research. And it is the agency of the creative practice researcher that is of primary interest to me here. So far, intentionally; 'when I am thinking I am just over here ...'

* *But when I am over here, again, I have thought - in the past tense. My proposition has been formed and I denote without rhetoric, speculation or modification in train. Parenthesis is escaped from, I return to the surface and declaim; I claim a collapse of time into a declarative present. I am in the space of mainline grammar and narrative - I am of the story, in the play. When I am over here I need no apologia for my method: it is normative ...*

... Meantime, return here to the apron of the page. As the past tense of being over there indicates, there is a distance involved, a distance which is not evident in the critical space which I inhabit now. You might most poignantly feel this distance. From there, no longer are you the readership (viewer) *for* my parenthetical soliloquy. You are observers of the mainline narrative of the play. You no longer have the benefit of a private audience with a protagonist who takes time at one side of the mainline narrative to decipher or embellish the story, intimately, with you, in parenthesis. With me over there you can relax with my normative conventions: no need to become concerned by the demands of a deciphering or an embellishment. When over there, there *is a silence from over here*; there is no strategic, critical intervention by the concerned protagonist on your behalf. When fixed in the mainline of normative conventions I am an *enacted* being whose business is epilogue.

Research by creative practice is, amongst other things, in contrast to epilogic research denotations, an opportunity to engage in *strategic soliloquy*. Such creative practice presents the opportunity for the creative practice researcher to fall back from the position of mainline narrative into an engaged reflection 'on the proceedings thus far'. This soliloquy, crucially, has an engaged audience, with members beyond, hopefully, the institutional supervisory and examination team. As proper parenthesis entails, the practitioner must not lose sight of the grammar of his chosen mainline of inquiry whilst in parenthesis; the way back to *over there*

Ken Neil

should not be foreclosed - anacoluthia should be averted, it ought to remain the prerogative of the engaged viewer only. Creative practice research, when most acute, compels the researcher himself to lay bare the creative acts of thinking as they happen. He is compelled to report on the machinations of the play, on his own behalf - and also ours. Returning to the foregrounded thought of this re-enactment *here*: where might the creative practice researcher *be* in the process of strategic soliloquy? The corollary, of course, is the question; where might we *wish them to be* in relation to their chosen field of inquiry, their 'mainline narrative'? A sketched answer to these questions begins to describe the role of the agency of the creative practice researcher in the process of inquiry.

Perhaps the protagonist undertaking research by creative practice is necessarily and usefully caught in a form of limbo - a limbo, in the abstract, somewhere between where I am presently, in parenthesis, and where I have come from, the tier of declamation and denotation. Indeed, a key note here is to say that the creative practice researcher must be encouraged to shuttle between the mainline narrative of inquiry and the complex of parenthetical reflection, for *the reflection itself must not be allowed to supplant the mainline narrative*; the method of inquiry must not usurp its origin. In other words, the programme of research by creative practice must not spiral into a hyperreality of methodological, instrumental signs; the soliloquist, if effectively engaged in the drama of his inquiry, must be able to move in and out of the preserved *origin* and the *parenthetical sign-complex* (body of work) which he devises as the vehicle for the soliloquy. It is the moving between the two positions that gives the researcher by creative practice his unique position, an enactment that situates the researcher in a productive limbo. In short, the successful research project by creative practice places, and should *require*, the researcher to be in an 'enacting limbo'. Researching by creative practice should rightly be described by the present participle: it is at its very heart, *being in an enacting limbo*.

This 'being' is a troublesome but critical component of the creative practice researcher's project. Its presence and its enactment should not be seen as a belittling of the intellectual status of the parenthetical sign-complex - for it is intrinsically *of* the structures of that sign-complex. Attention to *being in the work* does not inevitably render research discoveries in this area embarrassingly subjective, the stereotypical contradistinction to the normative declarations from over there.

This point about 'subjective agency' I mention for the methods of the researcher by creative practice have been given, rightfully, legitimization with reference to the semiotic analyses of Deleuze and Guattari, by virtue of those methods being *rhizomatic* as opposed to *arborescent*.[1] One consequence of this strategy is the, to be expected, playing down of the effect of the agency of the author in the orchestration of the 'semiotic chains' within the creative practice researcher's body of work. This soliloquy proposes that the *being* of the creative agent in the mainline narrative and in the subsequent body of work could be recuperated with greater transparency than might be 'allowed' by a purely semiotical treatment of the creative practice research endeavour. Deleuze and Guattari indirectly tempt such a recuperation when they set out to establish clear water between the arborescent and the rhizomatic: 'The tree is filiation, but the rhizome is alliance, uniquely alliance. The tree imposes the verb "to be", but the fabric of the rhizome is the conjunctions, and...and...and...'.[2] Perhaps by attending to predetermined ('to be') elements of *being in* the complex of signs, the semiotic chains, the researcher by creative practice can prompt conjunctive departures which would otherwise be overlooked as human contaminants in the

1 See the seminal essay by Jim Mooney, *Research in Fine Art by Project: General Remarks Toward Definition and Legitimation of Methodologies.*

2 Gilles Deleuze and Felix Guattari, *A Thousand Plateaus: Capitalism and Schizophrenia*, London: Athlone Press, 1998, p. 25.

3   Martin Heidegger, *Being and Time*, trans. J. Macquarrie and E. Robinson, Oxford: Blackwell, 1962.

4   Stephen Mulhall, *Heidegger and Being and Time*, London: Routledge, 1996, p. 30 (my emphasis).

semiotic laboratory. Once more, the productive limbo of being between here and there can be conducive to the researcher accounting for his *presence* as an agent in both the *origin* and the *parenthetical reflection*. This can be proposed flippantly: the productive limbo can be conducive to the researcher seeing himself in both the 'elements which are causally to be' (perhaps a Modernist existential aspect - *arborescent*) and in the 'elements which are casually at sea' (perhaps a Postmodernist aspect of privileging language over intrinsic *being - rhizomatic*).

I want to now speculatively embellish this *being in* positional limbo with fleeting reference to Heidegger's concept of *dasein*. An apologia for the creative work in limbo - between the mainline narrative and the edge of parenthesis - might well be found within existing discourse on intentional acts of inquiry and the self which intends these inquiries. One such discourse can be found in Heidegger's *Being and Time* (1927)[3] and it can assist in the recuperation of the being of the creative practice researcher in the process of research by creative practice. This kind of assistance is timely, at least in the terms of this parenthetical tangent, for it helps to redress the balance between the (troublesome) human agency and the (scientific) semiotic structures within the creative practice researcher's output. The *agency* installs a needed and healthy complexity to the parenthetical sign system - it re-enchants the body of work, and emphasizes its unique discursive status.

There is no question that Heidegger's philosophy of *dasein* is complex. My incomplete use of aspects of this philosophy may seem like a blatant act of anacoluthia, a perfect non-sequitur, and not a strategic parenthetical reflection, but the 'diversion' might shed light on aspects of the theme of 'agency'. As we know, in *Being and Time* Heidegger approaches fundamental ontological problems; one of which arises from the intentional relation between 'being' and 'an inquiry into being itself'. Any 'research into', any inquiry, must have a degree of intention or direction. Although answers are not always known in advance - the inquirer must hold some idea of intention. As the conference recognized implicitly, *any inquiry is an activity*; it is an enactment, the playing out of thinking. To place this reminder in Heideggerian discourse, 'any inquiry is an activity and that activity is engaged in by a particular kind of being'. Therefore, as the enactment of the inquiry unfolds, something of the particularity of the being of the inquirer will infiltrate the inquiry. As this essay has maintained thus far, we cannot have a presuppositional starting point for an inquiry. The predetermined aspects of the inquirer's self, and subsequent traces of the inquirer's self, when, and only if, *unearthed* in the *origin* of the inquiry can come to constitute the profoundly and perceptively critical output of the research by creative practice. Stephen Mulhall sees this 'awareness of the awareness of the inquirer in the inquiry' in Heidegger's own writing:

It is this sort of heightened self-awareness that is the most distinctive aspect of Heidegger's work; his investigation is permeated with an awareness of its own presuppositions. First, he makes explicit from the outset the pre-conceptions about his subject-matter that are orienting his analysis; they are not left in obscurity to be unearthed by disciples and exegetes, *but are themselves made the subject of analysis - an analysis which identifies the essential role of such preconceptions in any inquiry.*[4]

Heidegger acknowledges this characteristic of the 'human (humanist?) inquirer', and sees it as a vital idiosyncracy of the species - not a contaminant, but a necessary complexity of any successful analysis. He classifies the *very being of* human kind *as dasein*, for 'human kind is the kind of being for whom enquiring about entities with regard to their being is one possibility of *its* being'.

Ken Neil

What ought to be expected in substantive research by creative practice, at least according to this aside, is that the being of the inquirer (that being who has an impulse to inquire of ontological being on behalf of himself and others) is attended to in parenthetical moments of critical reflection on the mainline narrative of inquiry. What Heidegger tells us, on one count, is that there is a *necessariness* inherent in the term *dasein*: it is a necessary addition to the discourse of ontology because it 'sets out' to apprehend something previously 'felt' but not 'known' - that is, the awareness of the inquirer of his own agency omnipresent with-in and with-out the specifics of the inquiry. The term for Heidegger is necessary in describing, enigmatically, the being which precedes the inquiry into being. The necessariness of *dasein* validates the attention paid by the creative practice researcher to his 'being in the work', and also goes some way to legitimize the overarching process of the creative practice researcher's enactment of thinking. By this I mean that the *manifestation* of discoveries of both traces of the self and predetermined instances of the self in the origin of inquiry generously *makes available* a critical existential *and* semiotic thesis of, potentially, great academic utility; notwithstanding the potential of such work to be, in addition, stimulating and uplifting as a *thing in itself*. In being both a) critically informative about the happenings in the mainline narrative and b) in its own right an impressive soliloquy, the oeuvre of the creative practitioner can transcend the temporality of the specific mainline narrative, the stylistics of the soliloquy *and* the local particularities of the being of the inquirer. This outcome is unachievable if the dialectical conflation of *origin* and *particular being in the work* is neglected in favour of the fetishization of method.

To speak of the creative inquirer having, unavoidably as *dasein* instructs, *being in the work*, is subtly and crucially different from announcing, as the new art historians did, that one's interpretation of a body of work, or *origin* of inquiry, is dependent on the contingencies of the being of the beholder. *Dasein* has being in *both* enactments: both in here and over there. The creative inquirer inhabits an enacting limbo - they attend to the 'being' of the mainline narrative, the intentional object of their inquiry, and they attend to the evidence of self and trace of self; their being inhabits the *origin* and the *soliloquy* and the manifestation of the conflation (the body of work, the research output visual and textual). In this dialectic, the creative inquirer is involved not only in heuristics with regard to the mainline inquiry, they are involved in an ontological attempt to see themselves - their being playing itself out over here and over there. This activity produces a body of work which depends on the visually creative reflective qualities of the artist, and which lays bare the mainline narrative and the inquirer's being in the work.

Finally, we should be made aware, as the audience of the creative practice researcher's output, of a metaposition, a condition of *dasein* which reveals itself through the particular interplay between these two positions; here and there. We should welcome limbo in our own critical reception of the creative researcher's body of work; we should delight in being allowed to fall between the reality of the object of inquiry and the person-specific reflections of the inquirer. For then, in the spirit of microcosmic enlightenment and in the manner of the processions of signs to significations, we can adopt the output as 'thought', place it over there on the researcher's behalf and, subsequently, perpetuate the inquiry indefinitely, by attending to this thought in yet more parenthetical imaginings and reflections ...

* *...but anyway, to return to declamation ...*

Breaking the Circles of Uncertainty

Malcolm Miles

Abstract

This text asks if the notion of an avant-garde in art is viable today. It does this firstly with reference to recent (post-1967) theoretical and critical writing on avant-gardes in Europe in the nineteenth and twentieth centuries; and secondly, more indirectly, via questions in radical philosophy on the possibilities for radical social change. Perhaps to expect radical change today, or to foresee contemporary art as contributing to it, is forlorn, like waiting for Godot. Perhaps Beckett's violent gesture at the end of Waiting for Godot, when the characters walk on the spot, is as much as can be said, which is almost to refuse to say anything. And yet, while there is contemporary art, even at the margins, which engages on issues of social and environmental justice, and sees these as integral to each other, the effort to recover something of the hope once expressed by Courbet that art can change the world may yet be worthwhile.

Introduction

1 See J. Trowell, (2000), 'The Snowflake in Hell and the Baked Alaska: Improbability, Intimacy and Change in the Public Realm', in S. Bennett. and J. Butler (eds.) (2000), *Locality, Regeneration & Divers[c]ities*, Bristol: Intellect, pp. 99-109; M. Cornford and D. Cross (2001), 'Live Adventures', in I. Borden, J. Kerr, J. Rendell and L. Pivaro (eds.) (2001), *The Unknown City: Contesting Architecture and Social Space*, Cambridge, Mass.: MIT, pp. 328-39; M. Miles (2001), 'Viral Art - strategies for a new democracy', *Journal of Visual Art Practice*, vol. 1, no. 2, pp. 71-79.

Orthodox Marxism clung to the idea that there is an objectively given end of history. Despite being scientific in method, the idea is quite religious, and enables the revealers of that end to take on a priestly quality. The difficulty is that, of course, there is no such end guaranteed. And, less obviously but more importantly, if there was it would diminish the scope of struggle to achieve its ends and, crucially, limit the possibilities for participation of the supposed beneficiaries of radical change in determining its direction and form. This text is a brief foray into that terrain, seeking to investigate the problem of the avant-garde in art via an equivalent problem in radical philosophy. It refrains from presenting answers but, perhaps, conveys some sense of hope.

The aim of this text is, then, to ask if the notion of an avant-garde in art is viable today, firstly in terms of theoretical and critical writing on avant-gardes in Europe in the nineteenth and twentieth centuries; and secondly in terms of another question on the possibility of radical social change. It may be that to expect radical change today, or to foresee contemporary art as contributing to it, is forlorn, like waiting for Godot. And yet, while there is contemporary art, even at the margins, which engages on issues of social and environmental justice,[1] the effort to recover something of the hope once expressed by Courbet that art can change the world seems worthwhile.

The text begins by summarizing ideas of what constitutes an avant-garde - as anti-art, or as a political force in culture. It sees the failure of the avant-garde, as a concept, in its role as forerunner and revealer, positing both a privileged status for art and a notion of change as a process in time. This has certain parallels with a difficulty in the liberation discourse of the late 1960s, in which revolution depends on an awareness of the need for revolution which is itself a product of revolution - a circle which cannot be broken. The text proposes that by shifting the ground of the problem from time to space, however, a possibility is opened into moments within

JVAP 2 (1&2) 18–25 ©Intellect Ltd 2002

everyday life which already embody liberation - here and now, not there tomorrow. Finally, the text looks to Paolo Freire's *Pedagogy of the Oppressed* (1972), grounded in his work in adult literacy programmes in Brazil in the 1960s, for an alternative critical model from which present practices might learn.

Avant Gardes

There have been several avant-gardes in European and North American art histories. The most pervasive use of the term in Western art history and criticism denotes an anti-art movement within modernism.[2] This begins in the first decades of the twentieth century with movements such as Futurism and Dada; and with Duchamp's readymades. Just as the Futurists reject the art of the past, so the exhibition – as art – of an unadapted, industrially-produced object refuses art's convention of a privileged voice representing a privileged taste derived from a privileged social position. Although they differ in much, Duchamp, Dada, and the Futurists all retaliate against art's institutional baggage. This does not lead, however, to other commonalities. In the case of Zurich and Berlin, Dada there is a radicalism which, post-1918, informs, for instance, John Heartfield's anti-fascist montages, while those Futurists who survived the 1914-18 war supported fascism. Can they both be avant-garde? If so it seems to be a polyvalent concept.

Marinetti claims in his 'Manifesto of Futurism' that '... the world's magnificence has been enriched by a new beauty: the beauty of speed'.[3] Apart from retaining a bourgeois concept of beauty, this has an eschatological nuance which is linked, increasingly in Italy after 1918, to a myth of national regeneration. Emilio Gentile argues that:

> Many myths of the modernist avant-garde flowed into fascism and contributed to its ideology ... the element of symbiosis between culture and politics was the myth of national regeneration ... The myth of national regeneration can coexist with either nationalism or socialism, liberalism or totalitarianism. It can fit into a reformist and rationalistic concept of politics, but presents itself more often in revolutionary and eschatological forms. National regeneration is often messianic ...[4]

Similarly, Ernst Bloch observes in his critique of the rise of fascism and its relation to high and popular cultures in Germany, that it is the adrenalin of the apocalyptic which appeals especially to the petit-bourgeois class.[5] Whether it is as the end of one beauty and beginning of another, or as tales of lost crowns in the Rhine, is a detail.

So, if an attack on art's institutions is an attack by proxy on bourgeois society, it may just as easily be a proclamation of the last days having a contrasting political inference. This may stem, too, from the earliest developments of a distinctly and self-consciously modernist art. Hal Foster writes:

> Early modern art was partly adversarial: whether a dandy or a criminal (the two modern types as seen by Baudelaire), in pseudo-aristocratic withdrawal or radical transgression, the avant-gardist was posed against bourgeois culture.[6]

Much agonizing in twentieth-century cultural theory (including on the part of this writer) concerns justification for withdrawal as affording critical distance; but for

2 See for examples: R. Poggioli (1968), *The Theory of the Avant-Garde*, Cambridge, Mass.: Harvard University Press; P. Bürger (1984), *Theory of the Avant-Garde*, Minneapolis: University of Minnesota Press; R. Williams (1989), *The Politics of Modernism*, London: Verso.

3 'Manifesto of Futurism', first published in *Le Figaro*, Paris, 20 February 1909, reprinted in C. Harrison and P. Wood (eds.) (1992), *Art in Theory 1900-1990*, Oxford: Blackwell, pp. 145-49.

4 E. Gentile (1997), 'The Myth of National Regeneration in Italy: From Modernist Avant-Garde to Fascism', in M. Affron and M. Antliff (eds.) (1997), *Fascist Visions: Art and Ideology in France and Italy*, Princeton: Princeton University · Press, pp. 25-45.

5 E. Bloch (1991), *Heritage of Our Times*, Cambridge: Polity, see especially pp. 39-96.

6 H. Foster (1985), *Recodings: Art, Spectacle, Cultural Politics*, Seattle: Bay Press, p. 25.

7 Bürger, p. 109 n. 4.

8 Bürger, p. 53.

9 Bürger, p. 17.

10 E. Bloch [1938],
'Discussing
Expressionism', and G.
Lukács [1938], 'Realism
in the Balance', both in
Bloch et al. (1980),
Aesthetics and Politics,
London: Verso, pp. 16-
59.

11 See W. Kandinsky
[1911], Concerning the
Spiritual in Art, in
Harrison and Wood,
pp. 87-94, p. 89.

12 See O.K. Werckmeister
(1984), The Making of
Paul Klee's Career 1914-
20, Chicago: University
of Chicago Press, pp.
11-34.

13 Williams, p. 52, and in
Harrison and Wood, p.
147.

14 ibid.

avant-gardes the dichotomy of withdrawal and engagement seems to offer, in some cases, some nasty consequences. To differentiate avant-gardes, then, becomes a necessity.

But what differentiations? One such is obviously between Futurism and Dada, the former complicit in the violence of the fascist squads, the latter ridiculing fascism and exposing its economic context. This suggests, though, a difficulty in the argument advanced by Peter Bürger in *Theory of the Avant-Garde*. For Bürger, the avant-garde which attacks art's institutions is *the* avant-garde. While he mentions it only in passing, while making several references to Dada, Duchamp, and Heartfield, Bürger's definition of the avant-garde includes Futurism:

> The concept of the historical avant-garde movements used here applies primarily to Dadaism and early Surrealism but also and equally to the Russian avant-garde after the October revolution. ... a common feature ... is that they do not reject individual artistic techniques and procedures of earlier art but reject that art in its entirety, thus bringing about a radical break with tradition. In their most extreme manifestations, their primary target is art as an institution such as it has developed in bourgeois society. ... this is also true of Italian Futurism and German Expressionism.[7]

Bürger's main point is that the avant-garde negates individual production *and* reception in Dada performance, so that 'It is no accident that both Tzara's instructions for the making of a Dadaist poem and Breton's for the writing of automatic texts have the character of recipes', and 'All that remains is the individual who uses poetry as an instrument for living one's life ...'.[8] Something of that might accrue to Futurist performances, and is key to *agit-prop* in Russia. But Futurism and Expressionism still have uneasy relations to a rejection of bourgeois society. After all, Marinetti's ownership of a motor car marks him out, at that time, as a member of the bourgeois class. Bürger argues that 'In bourgeois society, it is only with aestheticism that the full unfolding of the phenomenon of art became a fact, and it is to aestheticism that the historical avant-garde movements respond';[9] which may be so, but the point is their responses are not alike.

The case of Nolde's affiliation to the Nazi state which then forbids him to make his pictures may be too easy an example of ambiguous politics, but as the dispute on Expressionism between Bloch and Lukács elucidates,[10] the categorization of Expressionism as a degenerate art does not mean it is necessarily anti-fascist art. Bloch's defence of it rests perhaps too much on this negative categorization, and enables him to ignore Kandinsky's anti-socialism,[11] and Franz Marc's vision in 1914 of the approaching war as a healthy purging of society[12] (as it was for the Futurists). Raymond Williams provides a clearer analysis. Citing the Futurist claim, again from Marinetti's manifesto of 1909, to sing of ' ... great crowds excited by work, by pleasure, and by riot' and ' ... multi-coloured, polyphonic tides of revolution in the modern capitals',[13] he argues that although Futurism overlaps in time with the rise of workers' movements, it is 'a world away from the tightly organized parties which would use a scientific socialism to destroy the hitherto powerful and emancipate the hitherto powerless'; and that 'there is the decisive difference between appeals to the tradition of reason and the new celebration of creativity which finds many of its sources in the irrational ... '.[14] For Williams, the gap between organized labour and an avant-garde of marginal status widens in the twentieth century. In contrast,

Malcolm Miles

Bürger says that 'The avant-garde intends the abolition of autonomous art by which is meant that art is to be integrated into the praxis of life',[15] and accepts that this cannot happen within a bourgeois society. But he gives no indication as to how anti-art, which he encapsulates in history, will realize this end. In a critical re-evaluation of Bürger's thesis, Ben Highmore notes that avant-gardism requires ' ... the transformation of art in the name of life and the transformation of life ... in the name of art', and that the avant-garde is (for Bürger) expressive of ' ... a certain frustration with the institutional conditions of art combined with the revolutionary desire to transform everyday life'.[16] He continues that Bürger misses the ambivalent relation to everyday life which characterizes both the anti-art avant garde *and* the art against which it reacts as something to be decried but also bearing a possibility of salvation.

The attitude of this avant-garde within modernism is a long way from Alan Kaprow's call for a critical reintegration of art and life:

> Contemporary artists are not out to supplant recent modern art with a better kind; they wonder what art might be. Art and life are not simply commingled; the identity of each is uncertain.[17]

What art *might* be! Or, for Joseph Beuys, the idea that everyone is an artist. This, too, could be apocalyptic, and perhaps that is an aspect of Beuys' self-mythologizing. But Kaprow's uncertainty - in the context of ephemeral, anti-commodification art such as happenings - conveys a sense of the dialogic.

The idea of political struggle characterizes an earlier formulation of an avant-garde. In an essay on the origin of the avant-garde in France, Linda Nochlin cites a passage from Henri de Saint-Simon in which a dialogue takes place between an artist and a scientist. The artist proclaims:

> It is we artists who will serve you as avant-garde ... the power of the arts is in fact most immediate and most rapid; when we wish to spread new ideas among men [sic], we inscribe them on marble or on canvas ... What a magnificent destiny for the arts is that of exercising a positive power over society, a true priestly function, and of marching forcefully in the van of all intellectual faculties ... .[18]

Nochlin next cites a passage from the Fourierist critic Laverdant:

> Art, the expression of society, manifests, in its highest soaring, the most advanced social tendencies; it is the forerunner and the revealer. Therefore to know whether art worthily fulfils its proper mission as initiator, whether the artist is truly of the avant-garde, one must know where Humanity is going, know what the destiny of the human race is ... .[19]

For Nochlin, Courbet's *The Painter's Studio* (1855) - a representation of Fourier's utopian socialism - is the epitome of this first avant-garde. Later in her essay she argues, however, that ' ... if we take "avant-garde" out of its quotation marks ... what is generally implied by the term begins with Manet rather than Courbet',[20] as a product of alienation. Courbet struggles in hope. Manet despairs. As Nochlin says, with Manet the matter is more complex than with Courbet's cultivation of a peasant

15 Bürger, pp. 53-54.

16 B. Highmore (2000), 'Awkward Moments: Avant-Gardism and the Dialectics of Everyday Life', in D. Scheunemann (ed.) (2000), *European Avant-Garde: New Perspectives*, Amsterdam: Rodopi, pp. 245-65.

17 A. Kaprow [1966], *Essays on the Blurring of Art and Life*, ed. J. Kelley (1993), Berkeley: University of California Press, p. 82.

18 H. de Saint-Simon [1825], *Opinions littéraires, philosophiques et indus-trielles*, cited in L. Nochlin (1967), 'The Invention of the Avant-Garde: France, 1830-80', in T.B. Hess and J. Ashbery (eds.) (1967), *Avant-Garde Art*, New York: Macmillan, p. 5.

19 G.-D. Laverdant [1845], *De la mission de l'art et du rôle des artistes*, in Nochlin, p. 6. Nochlin cites Saint-Simon from D.D. Egbert, 'The Idea of an "Avant-Garde" in Art and Politics', *The American Historical Review*, vol. 73, no. 2, December 1967, p. 343; and Laverdant from a slightly longer quote in Poggioli, *The Concept of the Avant-Garde*, published in Italian in 1962, p. 9.

20 Nochlin, p. 18.

21 Nochlin, p. 21.

22 J. Roberts (2001), 'Art, Politics and Provincialism', *Radical Philosophy*, no. 106, pp. 2-6.

23 H. Marcuse (1968), 'Liberation from the Affluent Society', in D. Cooper (ed.) (1968), *The Dialectics of Liberation*, Harmondsworth: Penguin, pp. 175-92.

24 Kaprow, p. 116.

25 H. Marcuse (1970), *Five Lectures*, Harmondsworth: Penguin, p. 80.

manner; his work embodies ' … his own essential feeling of alienation … a dandyish coolness toward immediate experience … '.[21] From this pervasive condition of art comes a remoteness even in politically conscious art. John Roberts writes:

> Political art … assumes that those whom the artwork is destined for … need art in as much as they need Ideas in order to understand capitalism … There is never … recognition that people are already engaged in practices … which are critical and transformative.[22]

Which draws attention, too, to the temporal frame in which freedom is located in a tomorrow which never dawns.

The End of Utopianism

In July 1967, Herbert Marcuse lectured at the Free University in Berlin, spoke at the Dialectics of Liberation Congress at the Roundhouse, London, and met the Vietnamese peace delegation in Paris. It might have seemed then that a new consciousness was dawning. To some of his listeners, rolling their own cigarettes, it might have been as nigh as for Timothy Leary with his mushrooms, or at Woodstock. In his Roundhouse paper Marcuse introduced the idea of society as a work of art,[23] meaning an ending of scarcity and libidinization of social relations, a society in which alienation is replaced by joy. There is an echo here of Fourier, for whom labour becomes libidinized sociation. Kaprow, too, writes that 'if all the secular world's a potential playground, the one taboo against playing is work. Work … must be replaced by something better … the concept of work is incompatible with that of play, childlike or holy'.[24] In North America there were happenings, and acts of sabotage by the Weathermen; in Paris, the Situationists wrote Lefebvre's words on the streets, and a link between students and workers promised revolution. But it never happened, and the failure was more than of tactics.

There is a difficulty in the concept of social transformation inherited from a modernity which had not yet ended, and in some ways parallel to the difficulty of the idea of an avant-garde. At the end of Marcuse's lecture 'The End of Utopia', a questioner says:

> … the centre of your paper today was the thesis that a transformation of society must be preceded by a transformation of needs … this implies that changed needs can only arise if we first abolish the mechanisms that have let the needs come into being as they are. It seems … you have shifted the accent toward enlightenment and away from revolution.

Marcuse replies:

> You have defined what is unfortunately the greatest difficulty in the matter … for new, revolutionary needs to develop, the mechanisms that reproduce the old needs must be abolished. In order for the mechanisms to be abolished, there must first be a need to abolish them. That is the circle in which we are placed, and I do not know how to get out of it.[25]

For the new society to come into being, the need for its realization must previously be felt as a new consciousness; only then can established institutions, including

Malcolm Miles

ideas, be demolished; yet the burden and possibility of creating that need, that consciousness, are situated in a realm not yet brought into being. But if the work of creating the preconditions in which future transformation can take place is located in that very transformation, then as Marcuse says, there is no way out of the dilemma. In *An Essay on Liberation* (1969), Marcuse extends this idea to a more or less biological force, arguing that awareness of that potential for freedom produced by technological advance itself produces a liberating consciousness. But, leaving aside that this may be no more than speculation, the liberation he imagines is projected onto a future towards which it is necessary to find a path. And the finding of the path is a matter of an interpreted reality.

The role of the avant-garde - or as Marcuse sees it the intelligentsia - is to undertake that interpretation. From this follows the notion of the University, or perhaps the Art School, as a safe house in an occupied land (though the Art School has conventionally been safer for men than for women).

Marcuse's model of liberation integrates Marxism and psychoanalysis, and goes a long way to dealing with the contradictions inherent in modernity, but it does not depart from a privileging of the new which in effect denies its presence in ordinary acts of dwelling. This brings the argument to the duality of critical distance, a key concept for Marcuse after the failure of revolution in Berlin in 1918 and again in the student protest movements in Paris and the US in 1968, both of which he experienced at first hand. The duality is that if the subject looks on a world imagined as other than it is, this is simultaneously and unavoidably an engagement with and a separation from that world. In the face of an unrelentingly grim political reality, the aesthetic dimension is where another world, qualitatively different from the world around, can be conceived but not perceived. Distance enables radical imagination but it means the world imagined is separated off, like art, from the world which changes. Yet the danger of an aestheticization of politics is demonstrated in fascism. In his earlier work, Marcuse points to the difficulties of what he terms affirmative culture; but in his later work it seems something not so far from it is what is left.

The relation of art's aesthetic and social dimensions in Marcuse's *Aesthetic Dimension* (1978) is similar, if more succinctly, to that presented by Adorno in *Aesthetic Theory*, incomplete on his death in 1969. Adorno has no optimism:

> Every artwork today, the radical ones included, has its conservative aspect; its
> existence helps to secure the spheres of spirit and culture, whose real
> powerlessness and complicity with the principle of disaster becomes plainly
> evident ... Artworks are ... socially culpable ... Their possibility of surviving
> requires that their straining towards synthesis develop in the form of their
> irreconcilability.[26]

Art's aesthetic and social dimensions are mutually erasing, though this represents not gloom but an effort to keep the argument open.

To sum up: successive avant-gardes demonstrate ambivalence in their relation to social processes in general and to progressive positions on social organization. This derives from a withdrawal, from the 1870s in Paris, to an autonomous aesthetic dimension which offers critical distance but disables intervention. A further problem, pre-dating the first, is that the role even of a progressive avant-garde depends on a separation of art from life: an interpretation of the world for others;

26 T.W. Adorno (1997), *Aesthetic Theory*, London: Athlone Press, p. 234.

27 For instance, H.
   Lefebvre (1991), *The
   Production of Space*,
   Oxford: Blackwell.

28 P. Freire (1972),
   *Pedagogy of the
   Oppressed*,
   Harmondsworth:
   Penguin, pp. 18-19.

29 Freire, p. 25.

and a projection of the revealed freedom onto a future remote from a present seen, reciprocally, as devoid of freedom. Marcuse's unbreakable circle in which tomorrow never comes because it is not today mirrors avant-garde art's circle of a tomorrow which can only be imagined, is never realized and never here.

Common to both is a refusal to accept, because it would wreck art's and philosophy's privileged status, that moments of liberation permeate routine, are here now even if in marginalized areas of life.

Another Ground

This is where Henri Lefebvre's writing[27] has much to offer, because it recognizes that sense of the everyday which is not void. If the ground of the problem approached by Marcuse in his Berlin lecture in 1967 is shifted from time to space, and to a space of everyday lives in which there are glimpses of liberation, then liberation is immanent (pervasive) not imminent (looming). It offers a way out of the circle by relocating the dreamed-of freedom in a present where it requires not to be imagined or revealed, but recognized. Then the difficulty is to overcome the marginalization of embodied hope by the dominant society and its cultural institutions, so that society really is a work of art and play. Crucial to the undertaking is an equality of status among the participants, and in this respect more radical thought and practice may be found in fields such as liberation ecology, and work in the non-affluent world, than in the cultural or academic institutions of the affluent world. This text turns, finally, as a long-established case of such thought, to Paolo Freire.

Commenting on the myth-making and irrationality of sectarianism, Freire writes in *Pedagogy of the Oppressed*, first published in Portuguese in 1967:

> The radical, committed to human liberation, does not become the prisoner of a 'circle of certainty' ... On the contrary, the more radical he [sic] is, the more fully he enters into reality so that, knowing it better, he can better transform it.[28]

Freire's ideas were formed in his experiences in adult literacy programmes in Brazil from the 1940s onwards, for which he was arrested and exiled in 1964, and in UN agrarian reform projects in Chile after that. In 1969, Freire was appointed to a post at Harvard, then moved to Geneva in 1970 to work for the World Council of Churches as a consultant on Africanization in Tanzania and Guinea-Bissau. He returned to Brazil in 1980.

The framework of Freire's ideas is postcolonial liberation. In recognition of the value of local knowledge in the face of the environmental destructiveness of economic colonialism, liberation ecology extends this. But a key element in Freire's pedagogy came from his practice of adult literacy education:

> The central problem is this: how can the oppressed, as divided, unauthentic beings, participate in developing the pedagogy of their liberation? Only as they discover themselves to be 'hosts' of the oppressor can they contribute to the midwifery of their liberating pedagogy. As long they live in the duality where to be is to be like, and to be like is to be like the oppressor, this contribution is impossible.[29]

The model of colonialism is that of subject-object, in which one party draws up the rules of the game and determines what are the allowed and disallowed ways in which others play. The rules are introjected through culture so that the objectified colonial subject is self-coercing, seeking to be like the colonial power, which, as Freire says, is always impossible.

Colonial power is maintained by ensuring that local knowledges are counted as dirt. This reproduces the pedagogy of formal education, from the nineteenth century, in the imperial countries. In this, those who teach pass on a body of knowledge more or less coercively to those they take as empty receptacles for it. Freire terms this the banking concept of education. He writes that when 'knowledge is a gift bestowed by those who consider themselves knowledgeable upon those whom they consider to know nothing' the absolute ignorance projected onto others negates education as a process of inquiry.[30] The banking concept of education, like Victorian charity, ensures the status of the donor by requiring the gratitude of the recipient. Freire proposes instead an equality of exchange between teacher and student which respects the different but equivalent knowledge of both, in a dialectic not hierarchic relation. This interrupts power by de-centring it. Change in this scenario is produced in a process in which people free themselves. There is no longer an avant-garde.

But, as the purpose of this text is to recover something, particularly from the earlier, politicized idea of an avant-garde, it does not end in that bleak statement which is also filled with hope. This is not to say that any specific category of art - say, the new-genre public art proposed by Suzanne Lacy[31] - has answers. Adorno's distrust of solutions can be remembered here. But there are critical art practices today in which power is ruptured. To end, then, the text cites one example in the work of Mierle Ukeles. In *Cleaning of the Mummy Case* at the Wadsworth Athenaeum in Hartford, Connecticut (1973), Ukeles redesignated a glass case as art: a gesture which intersects the power relations of the museum in which cleaners are allowed to clean cases but only conservators can touch art. The elite end up doing manual work, cleaning the glass case. It does not improve the wages or working conditions of the 'real' cleaners mopping the floors while they do it, but problematizes the issue of hierarchy, intervening in the linguistic categories which condition power relations. Patricia Phillips observes: 'If sinks were declared art objects, for instance, would conservators become the guardians of public washrooms?'[32] A nice thought. And a serious one, not unrelated to Gandhi's idea that everyone, regardless of status, should do at least one hour of manual work each day. His own was spinning.

In conclusion, the concept of an avant-garde as leading the wider society from today to tomorrow is not viable. It involves acts of revelation or interpretation for others - who are in fact fully able if given the chance to interpret the world for themselves, which act is itself a beginning of liberation. Freire writes that 'Cooperation, as a characteristic of dialogical action ... can only be achieved through communication ... there is no place for conquering the people on behalf of the revolutionary cause ... '.[33] But this does not preclude acts of provocation which undermine structures of power and lend visibility to manifestations of present hope.

30 Freire, p. 42.

31 S. Lacy (1995), *Mapping the Terrain*, Seattle: Bay Press.

32 P. Phillips (1995), 'Maintenance Activity', in N. Felshin (ed.) (1995), *But Is It Art?*, Seattle: Bay Press, pp. 165-94.

33 Freire, p. 136.

Spatial ontology and digital print

Naren Barfield

Abstract

The author's 1999 doctoral submission, 'Integrated Artworks: Theory and Practice in relation to Printmaking and Computers, and the influence of 'non-Euclidean geometry' and 'the fourth dimension' on developments in Twentieth-Century Pictorial Space' examined relations between spatial art practice and theory, digital technology, print and photomechanical imaging methods, hyperspace philosophy and recent art-historical analyses of developments in pictorial space during the quarter-century preceding the First World War. This paper, presented at 'The Enactment of Thinking' conference at the University of Plymouth in July 2001, introduces aspects of this research and examines, specifically, ideas from geometry and hyperspace philosophy, and key terms including shadows, slices, projections and the dimensional analogy, to assist in understanding and visualizing historically significant but unconventional modes of spatial discourse. Examples of the author's work are included and help to relate theory to practice within the research.

Introduction

1. Anthony Quinton, 'Ontology', in Allan Bullock and Stephen Trombley (eds.), *The New Fontana Dictionary of Modern Thought*, 3rd edition, London: HarperCollins, 1999, p. 608-09.

2. Katy Macleod and Lin Holdridge, 'The Enactment of Thinking: creative practice research degrees', Introduction to the Conference, Exeter: University of Plymouth, 2001.

Ontology. The theory of existence or, more narrowly, of what really exists, as opposed to that which appears to exist but does not, or that which can properly be said to exist but only if conceived as some complex whose constituents are the things that really exist.[1]

So that is clear, then. It does, however, appear somewhat removed from the everyday concerns of the average visual artist, even one who might be engaged in doctoral research. Perhaps a more fruitful way of thinking about ontology in relation to artistic thought and practice is given by Katy Macleod and Lin Holdridge, who in their introduction to 'The Enactment of Thinking' conference (University of Plymouth, 2001), give the following description of the artist/researcher's thinking: 'This is thinking which is dependent on the artist's ontological speculations about being in the world according to her/his determining vision of it'.[2] This compact sentence is valuable as a description not only of the thinking of the artist/researcher in general, but as the starting point for the author's specific research concerns, which are located in the investigation of subjective space and persistent spatial problems and ideas using print, digital computer technology, construction and installation. Thus, the title of this paper - 'Spatial ontology and digital print' – refers to both the investigation of the concepts and experiences of space through the material practice of digital print, and the transforming influence of ontological speculation on the methods and processes of that material practice itself. Given this, one of the purposes of this paper is to attempt to illustrate how complex relations between theoretical knowledge and practice can result in new forms of practice where the physical artefact embodies theoretical knowledge, in turn

JVAP 2 (1&2) 26–35 ©Intellect Ltd 2002

providing a legitimate basis for doctoral-level work involving a substantial component of original creative practice.

Rationale

There are a number of reasons for this approach. Firstly, the author is a practising artist regularly working in both print and digital media, with a theoretical interest in the history and development of unconventional spatial discourses in fine art practice, particularly in the area of non-perspectival pictorial spaces, artistic applications of alternatives to three-dimensional Euclidean geometry, and the identification and utilization of alternative depth cues, as a means to investigating and expanding on issues of personal and subjective space.

Secondly, as computers have increasingly become a commonplace of fine art practice, it has become possible to raise questions more critical than heretofore regarding their incorporation into the range of media used by artists. Where once the focus was on attempts to 'discover' the properties and image-making potential of a new medium, it is now more appropriate - and, it might be argued, essential - to question what it is that is actually required of computer technology: in other words, how the technology might be used to serve the artist's 'ontological speculations' about their place in the world and their relations to it.

In this regard, it is important to remember that the majority of currently available digital imaging software applications have been developed primarily for commercial purposes, with the reprographic requirements of the graphic design and publishing industries uppermost. Consequently, as any artist appropriating the medium would discover, the imaging paradigms that they would encounter are more than likely to have been developed with respect to photography, montage, the idea of a 'window on the world', and verisimilitude: all modes of representational discourse borrowed from older, established practices, and with a range of spatial competences, applications and limitations.

The corollary of this is that the artist seeking a medium with which to mount their 'ontological speculations' may be compelled, when working digitally, to operate within the limitations of a potentially alien discourse which, through no fault of its own, bears little or no relation to the artistic or philosophical problems with which they might be concerned. The artist working with digital media may therefore face a choice: to learn, work within and make a positive feature of the discourse they are presented with; or alternatively, to learn to control and manipulate (and subvert from its given purpose) that discourse in the service of another discourse, centred on their own practice and research questions.

Before ideas about space can be explored through print and computer technology, however, it is essential to examine the ideas themselves, and the author's research has involved an extensive critical review of significant new evidence - by art historians Linda Dalrymple Henderson,[3] Craig Adcock,[4] Tom Gibbons[5] and others - linking the twentieth-century departure from the traditions of perspectival representation to the late nineteenth- and early twentieth-century popularity of 'alternative' space systems such as non-Euclidean and *n*-dimensional geometry, hyperspace philosophy and the idea of 'the fourth dimension', a concept which, in both its geometrical and philosophical interpretations, held great sway over artists in the early years of the twentieth century, and was more influential upon the discourses and development of modern art than has been generally recognized.

To return to the title of this paper, it can be asked: what is significant about

3. Linda Dalrymple Henderson, *The Fourth Dimension and Non-Euclidean Geometry in Modern Art*, Princeton: Princeton University Press, 1983.

4. Craig Adcock, *Marcel Duchamp's Notes from the "Large Glass": An N-Dimensional Analysis*, Studies in the Fine Arts, Avant-Garde, no. 40. Ann Arbor, Michigan: UMI Research Press, 1983.

5. Tom Gibbons, 'Cubism and "The Fourth Dimension" in the Context of the Late Nineteenth-Century and Early Twentieth-Century revival of Occult Idealism', *Journal of the Warburg and Courtauld Institutes*, vol. XXXXIV, The Warburg Institute, University of London, 1981.

6. Edwin Abbott Abbott, *Flatland, A Romance of Many Dimensions*, New Jersey: Princeton University Press, 1991.

7. Abbott, *op. cit.*, introduction, p. xvi. The slicing technique may be compared to modern radiologists' scans, where the three-dimensional 'picture' is built from planar cross-sections through the body.

spatial ontology explored through digital print, and what is the reason for its choice as a research subject? To pursue this: how does digital print examine and address issues of spatial ontology; and how does a spatially oriented art practice provide a framework for thinking about, and developing and extending practice and research in, digital print? An attempt at a workable rationale for such research, and a formal link between the two areas of spatial ontology, on the one hand, and digital print on the other, might be framed as follows.

Ontological speculation by the artist about their being in the world must, if they are 'embodied' (and this can be reasonably assumed, unless they are a 'virtual' artist operating in cyberspace), take account of their extension in space, a necessary property of physical or material existence. Ontological speculation that considers embodied existence must, therefore, consider spatially extended experience (and this experience is self-conscious; if the artist is able to make ontological speculations about being in the world, awareness of their own 'being-ness' must be self-conscious). *Spatial* ontology then can be described as: ontological speculation or inquiry/examination into or of self-conscious personal spatial extension, possibly in relation to external spatial phenomena or cues. *Spatial ontology* stands as shorthand for precisely this sort of speculative inquiry.

The relation of this to digital print is less immediately apparent, and provides much in the way of research questions and practical problems investigated in the author's own research. Such a relation is predicated on an existing or assumed relationship between digital (technology) and print(making), a relationship which, once a highly contentious area of dispute between traditionalists and advocates of the new, is now a firmly established area of creative practice. Taking *digital print* as a given for the purposes of this paper, then, examples of practical work will be used to show its relation to the speculative spatial inquiry outlined above.

A Different Space

To assist with the introduction of unconventional spatial concepts it might be helpful to attempt a brief thought experiment, derived from *Flatland*,[6] part social satire and part scientific speculation written in 1884 by Edwin Abbott Abbott, and still highly popular and regularly reprinted to this day. As the name suggests, *Flatland* is a realm limited to a two-dimensional planar existence which is visually unrewarding for its inhabitants, a population comprised of two-dimensional polygons unable to 'see' into a third dimension.

Become, temporarily, a *Flatlander*: what is it possible to see? In the absence of a third dimension, vision is possible only along the plane, and all you could see would be lines or edges, differentiated only by length and their varying degrees of brightness. Now, with these limitations to the visual field, how could you attempt to 'see', or appreciate, the existence of a third dimension. It is, of course, not directly possible in a world unable to contain volume, and an alternative must be sought. The method provided in *Flatland* is the 'slicing technique', where a 'picture' of the three-dimensional world is built up by the imagination from viewing a series of cross-sections through objects.[7] The 'slicing technique' could be employed, for example, to imagine a sphere passing through a plane. If you were a *Flatlander* observing this, you would see a point appearing as if from nowhere, expanding to a circle, and then shrinking again to a point before disappearing from view as mysteriously as it had appeared.

This thought experiment, which uses the dimensional analogy to imagine a third

Naren Barfield

dimension from a two-dimensional world, may be extended to imagine a fourth dimension. In this scenario, visited by a four-dimensional sphere, or hypersphere, you would observe a point appear in space, growing in time to a three-dimensional sphere which has the appearance of a globe floating in space, and subsequently diminishing again to a point before disappearing.

The slicing technique may be employed to attempt to visualize four-dimensional objects by observing a succession of three-dimensional cross-sections, as two-dimensional cross-sections may be used to visualize the three-dimensional object. Thus, just as a sphere may be regarded as a three-dimensional stack of circles, a hypersphere can be considered a four-dimensional stack of spheres.[8]

While the projection of a sphere onto a perpendicular plane produces a circle, or 'shadow', possessing no value in the third dimension, a sphere may itself be seen as an infinitesimally thin 'shadow' of a four-dimensional hypersphere, a 'projection' of a four-dimensional object into a three-dimensional space. Thus, as long as a form may be viewed as the shadow of a higher dimension, three-dimensional objects may perhaps be seen as mere shadows of some superior four-dimensional 'hyperforms'.[9]

This is implied romantically by Edwin Abbott Abbott in *Flatland*. As art historian Linda Dalrymple Henderson has written: 'Abbott's tale is based on the premise that the meaning of the third dimension for a two-dimensional being compares to the meaning of the fourth dimension for us.'[10] So, by dimensional analogy, four is to three as three is to two. Recent research has shown that speculations on the 'fourth dimension', and its frequent companion, 'non-Euclidean geometry' have played a role in the development of art more central than heretofore assumed.[11]

Having considered 'the fourth dimension', it may be helpful to attempt to elucidate its companion term, 'non-Euclidean geometry'. It may be considered self-evident that parallel lines do not meet. This appears to be a matter of common sense, but was given precise form in Euclid's fifth, or parallel, postulate,[12] which is perhaps best understood by its alternative definition: 'Through a given point one and only one straight line can be drawn which will be parallel to a given straight line', where it is assumed that the two lines are in the same plane and of infinite length.

The parallel postulate was subject to centuries of attempted proofs, including that of Gauss who, being unable to disprove its falsity, concluded that a 'non-Euclidean geometry' was possible, and that it did not contradict Euclid's geometry, but could in fact contain it. Gauss revealed his ideas to only a few friends, it falling upon Lobachevsky (in 1829-30) and Bolyai (in 1832) to publish the first accounts of a geometry independent of the parallel postulate.

The Lobachevsky-Bolyai geometry, held to be negatively curved and hyperbolic, departed from Euclid's parallel postulate, since it was possible for more than one line passing through a point not to touch a given line, and angle sums in triangles totalled less than 180°. A generation later, Riemann, a student of Gauss, introduced an alternative 'non-Euclidean geometry', in which space was positively curved and elliptic, parallel lines intersected, and angle sums in triangles totalled more than 180°.

Therefore, to revisit our two-dimensional world, how would you know if it were flat, or curved? For any point on your plane, the surrounding area would appear flat, and you could demonstrate this by inscribing a triangle in the ground, and measuring its angles, which would total 180°. If, however, your flat world was part of

8. Rudolf van B. Rucker, *The Fourth Dimension and How to Get There*, London: Penguin, 1986, p. 19.

9. Thus, a four-dimensional hypersphere is projected into three-dimensional space as a sphere which, when projected onto a two-dimensional surface, appears as a circle. If this circle is then pro-jected again it becomes a line in one dimension, and a point in zero dimensions. The artist Tony Robbin is strenuous on this subject, asserting, in effect, that *all* phenom-ena of the three-dimensional physical world presented to the senses can be re-cast as shadows of four-dimensional experience. Although Kant would never accept his four-dimen-sional interpretation, Robbin's position is essentially a parallel of the philosopher's *ding-an-sich*, the thing-in-itself which transcends experience, and is knowable to the senses only through the phenomenon. Indeed, for Robbin, the four-dimensional world *is* the noumenal reality, and not merely a con-venient or fascinating geometrical abstraction; it belongs to the experiential, not merely theoretical domain. To quote the relevant passage in full (where he also 'updates' the three-dimensional Plato to a four-dimensional

Einstein): 'Now, in Einstein's cave, the shadows we observe are three-dimensional; they have mass, exist in time, and obey physical laws. But these shadows, too, are phantasmagorical. Their shapes, masses, and internal clocks are different for just about every viewer, owing to relativistic effects. For some viewers, the physical attributes of the shadows are *vastly* different, and sprouts grow into huge oak trees that wither from old age in the time it takes to drink a cup of coffee. To be faithful to our philosophical traditions we should say that the four-dimensional, integral, symmetrical origins of these multiple and contradictory shadows are real and that this reality is presented to us via its projections. We must break the habit of considering four-dimensional entities to be merely artificial constructs used in physics' (Tony Robbin, Fourfield, *Computers, Art and the Fourth Dimension*, USA: Bullfinch Press, 1992, p. 38).

10. Linda Dalrymple Henderson, *The Fourth Dimension and non-Euclidean Geometry in Modern Art*, Princeton: Princeton University Press, 1983, p. 17.

11. See Henderson, 1983, *op. cit.*

12. 'If a straight line falling on two straight lines make the interior angles on the same

the surface of a spherical planet, and you attempted to use this method, you would notice that as your triangles became larger, so too did the sum of the angles, and if you were to measure a triangle which covered one quarter-hemisphere, you would observe its angles adding up to 270°, or three right-angles. Space, although flat to you, would be curved.[13]

The terms 'the fourth dimension', and 'non-Euclidean geometry' have often been used interchangeably. As hyperspace mathematician Tom Banchoff has observed, perhaps this is understandable:

> The ideas of non-Euclidean geometry became current at about the same time that people realised that there could be geometries of higher dimensions. Some observers lumped these two notions together and assumed that any geometry of dimension higher than three had to be non-Euclidean.[14]

It is possible, however, to have geometries of two, three, or higher dimensions, which are either Euclidean or non-Euclidean. Thus 'the fourth dimension', and 'non-Euclidean geometry' are distinct, but may be conjoined. Time, as opposed to space, is also often thought of as a fourth dimension, part of the space-time continuum, resulting from the work of Minkowski. While time is a fourth dimension, it does not replace the notion of the spatial fourth dimension, with which it is often confused.

Ideas such as these have provided artists over the past century with a rich range of spatial descriptions, and alternatives to conventional spatial discourse. Studies on depth perception in cognitive psychology[15] have also provided at least seven monocular, and three binocular, cues to the perception of depth. These also provide an expanded range of tools with which the artist can carry out their speculations about being in the world. Monocular cues include both *linear* and *aerial* perspectives (known, for obvious reasons, as *pictorial* cues, from which they are derived); *texture* (including changes in texture with distance from the viewer); *interposition* (where a distant object is occluded by a nearer one); *shading* (since two-dimensional surfaces do not cast shadows, shading is normally evidence of depth); *familiar size* (where retinal image size provides a guide to the estimation of distance); and *motion parallax* (the effect which describes the movement of an image over the retina, whether caused by the movement of the object, or of the viewer's eye). Binocular depth cues include both *accommodation* and *convergence*, as well as *stereopsis*, where a different image is produced on each retina, and from which depth may be estimated.

Spatial Practice

This section will consider briefly certain aspects of the author's visual arts practice which provide evidence for the claim that complex relations between theoretical knowledge and practice can result in new forms of practice where the physical artefact embodies theoretical knowledge; and that this in turn reflects both the investigation of the concepts and experiences of space through the material practice of digital print, and the transforming influence of ontological speculation on the methods and processes of that material practice itself.

Methods are presented for using computer technology to extend the traditionally two-dimensional print into physical space to create new types of large-scale sculpted, or *constructed* works which digitally integrate autographic drawing, photographic imagery, printmaking and modelling from architectural-type plan drawings.

Naren Barfield

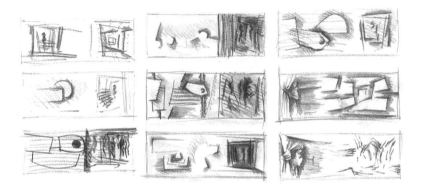

Figure 1: Sketches for development of small-scale maquettes.

Constructed Prints

The development of two-dimensional prints into larger-scale constructed pieces began with a series of sketches [figure 1] from which a number of small-scale maquettes were made using card, paper and other materials. Onto these, imagery (from sketches and photographs made on site) was drawn and painted by hand, to assist with judging the eventual position of the digital imagery on the larger-scale works.

From the more successful of the maquettes, accurate measurements of the structures were carefully taken for the creation of detailed drawings [figure 2], which

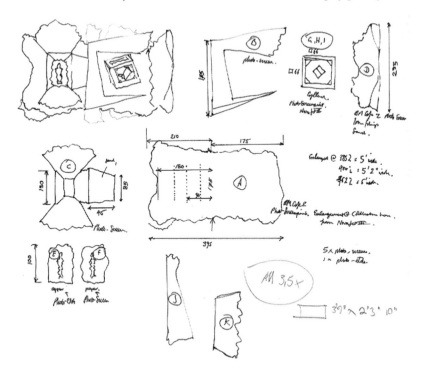

Figure 2: Example of drawings of separate components parts (with measurements) for developments of small-scale maquettes.

side less than two right angles, the two straight lines, if produced indefinitely, meet on that side on which are the angles less than the two right angles' (Postulate V, Heath's translation of Heiberg's text, Cambridge University Press, 1908, in Roberto Bonola, *Non-Euclidean Geometry*, New York: Dover Publications, 1955, p. 1, translated and with additional appendices by H.S. Carslaw).

13. See Thomas F. Banchoff, *Beyond the Third Dimension*, New York: Scientific American Library, 1990, p. 185. The work of Riemann showed that, provided space had a curvature of ever so small a positive value, then the Universe would not be infinite, but would be both finite and unbounded, like the surface of a sphere.

14. *ibid.*, p. 190.

15. Michael Eysenck, and Mark Keane, *Cognitive Psychology: A Student's Handbook*, 3rd ed., Hove, Erlbaum, UK: Taylor & Francis, 1995, p. 37ff.

were subsequently developed in to architectural-type plans using a vector-based 'constructed drawing' computer application [figure 3]. For this, each maquette was broken down into its separate component parts, or 'segments', each requiring an individual 'unfolded blueprint' from which the 'building blocks' for the eventual construction were made.

Photographs of the site, the interior of the British Museum in London, were taken using a simplified method developed previously, and were digitally combined using an image-manipulation application. The resulting composite images were adjusted to fit accurately the shapes of the 'unfolded' plan drawings. A third computer application (a page layout program) was then used for the combination and placement of images [figure 4]. The results were printed at a small scale, after which each component was cut out, folded and glued individually, before being bonded together, and the resulting constructions tested for accuracy of measurement and image placement.

Using these resulting constructions as working models, modifications were then made in the drawing and image-manipulation applications, and precise scaling up to full size achieved in the page layout program, before printing. The large-scale prints were cut, folded and glued. A foam core backing was used to strengthen the finished works [figure 5].

Although alternative methods were tested, such as using three-dimensional modelling software, and 'unfolding' utilities, the method described proved more effective in providing the flat form necessary for obtaining the printed output from which the constructions were eventually made.

Observations and relation to theory
Figures 5 and 6 contain a fully-modelled three-dimensional representation of a

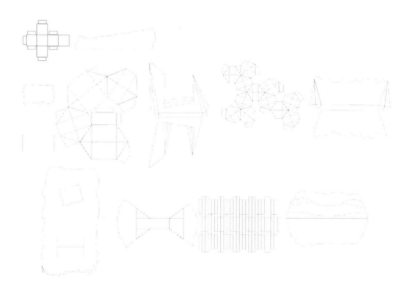

Figure 3. Architectural-type plans of separate component parts for development of small-scale maquettes, created using a vector-based 'constructed drawing' computer application (not to scale). These component parts are combined with imagery, cut, folded and glued.

Naren Barfield

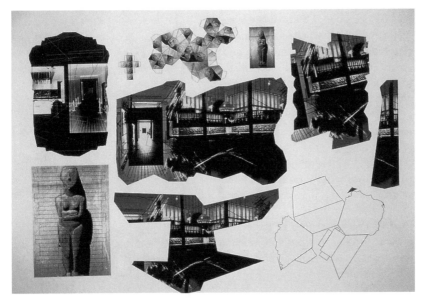

Figure 4. 'Unfolded' elements combined with digitally manipulated photographs to provide discreet components for cutting, gluing and construction.

projected hypercube (a four-dimensional cube) which was constructed using trigonometrical calculations so that the piece could be modelled accurately from a single piece of flat paper. The advantage of using a vector-based drawing application over traditional methods is that complicated drawings are easily modified and, being resolution-independent, are scalable without loss of detail, or risk of distortion. Additional advantages arise from the new methods developed here. The computer enables the pieces to be visualized prior to construction, allowing alternatives to be considered before a final choice is made. The small-scale maquettes can be produced in relatively less time than larger pieces, and corrections can be made at that stage; and scaling the component parts up or down

Figure 5. Final construction combining each of the discreet elements into a unified work.

is also easily done at the software stage. Additionally, accurately scaling, distorting and adjusting imagery to fit across the irregular surfaces of the constructed works would be extremely difficult to achieve using other means.

Due to the way in which large-scale works such as this function, they relate to a number of spatial issues earlier considered theoretically. Instead of more familiar depth cues to articulate the space, such as linear and aerial perspective, motion parallax and shading become central to the spatial reading, as does interposition, when at close range one part of the object occludes another.

Chair

The relations between theoretical knowledge and practice described above resulted in the development of new forms of practice which a later work,

Figure 6. Detail of final work showing how effects of motion parallax, shading and interposition become central to the spatial reading.

Chair [figure 7], was able to use to create an interplay between the simultaneous experiences of image and object as the viewer encounters the work. *Chair* explores issues of subjective space through a dialogue between dimensional analogies, and the idea of an object in one dimension being the shadow of the next higher spatial dimension.

Produced as a direct spatial intervention into the gallery, or viewer's own, environment, the work unites one (three-dimensional) half of an ordinary household chair with a photographically-originated two-dimensional image of its 'lost' half. This image can be read as both a reflection (as seen in a mirror), or as a shadow, indicating its inferior spatial dimensionality. When united in the viewer's perception, the two counterparts - the two- and three-dimensional halves - make the chair whole again, and the spatial experience is apparently complete. Additional shadows cast by the two-dimensional image, however, pose further spatial problems (the reason that an image and not a mirror is used, is that the shadows are permanently fixed and the 'reflection' is indifferent to the movement of the viewer in relation to the work), implying that the hierarchy of shadows may be taken symbolically to suggest an endless game of dimensional expansion.

Derived from, and designed to question, spatial problems arising from Kant's *Prolegomena*, Abbott's *Flatland*, Duchamp's *Large Glass*, the conceptual and spatial complexities of *Chair* required a number of approaches in its practical development and execution, including mathematically precise distortions of the scanned digital image of the photograph of the 'lost' half of the chair, in order to make it match the dimensions of the 'real' chair. Careful attention was also required to match the colour between the physical and the printed components under particular gallery and lighting conditions.

Naren Barfield

Summary and Conclusions

Awareness of developments in fields as diverse as art history, cognitive psychology and digital print technologies provides a rich field of inquiry in support of the artist's 'ontological speculations' about space and being in the world. New, synthetic methods have been generated through these relationships which make possible new forms of practice which are characterized, shaped by, and in turn embody theoretical knowledge concerned with unconventional spatial discourses and issues of personal and subjective space. The experience of practical investigation of these issues also provides insights and knowledge not derived by theoretical speculation, and analysis of this practical investigation in turn provides valuable information contributing to the body of theory.

Figure 7. Chair. *Chair (sawn in half), digitally manipulated photograph, mounted inkjet print. 50 x 100 x 30cm (approx).*

1 METHODOLOGICAL
EMBODIMENTS:
Psychical Corporeal
Performances of
Subjective Specific
Auto[erotic]-
Representation(s) is the
full title of the doctoral
thesis by Dr RyyA.
Bread©. The research
project was
successfully submitted
in July 2001 to
Falmouth College of
Arts, Cornwall; and val-
idated by the University
of Plymouth, Devon. A
copy of the dissertation
is housed in the library
of each of these institu-
tions and should be
made available upon
request. All
photographs included
in this text were gener-
ated between 1997 and
2001 by RyyA. Bread©
within the doctoral
research and used in
the thesis.

'Hue' am I?
A colour-[de]coding of RyyA. Bread©'s
METHODOLOGICAL EMBODIMENTS[1]

RyyA. Bread©

My goal is not to answer the question, 'Who am I?' but to identify a framework in which this question could make sense. (RyyA. Bread©)

That an entity is not the *causa sine qua non* does not proscribe against its being the *causa causans*. Observing light through a prism (though 'we know' that the prism is not the absolute origin of the resplendent spectacle before us) we do not deny its effect upon the light, still less call for the death of the prism. That the author can only be conceived as a manifestation of the Absolute Subject, this is the root message of every authocide. One must, at base, be deeply *auteurist* to call for the Death of the Author. (Burke 1992: 27)

From the prism that I have called *matrixial*, to the extent that 'woman' diffracts, she also digs channels of meaning and sketches an area of difference with sublimational outlets and ethical values paradoxical in the phallic paradigm. (Lichtenburg Ettinger 1996: 92)

Abstract

Colour is only one element in an elaborate methodological strategy that is deployed within my interdisciplinary praxis. Nonetheless, a colour-coding schema has emerged as an increasingly significant performative structural function within the formation of METHODOLOGICAL EMBODIMENTS. For this reason, it has been signalled out for the purposes of this text:

1. To provide a specific example of how an interplay between multiple 'visual-material' and 'linguistic' practices are mediated through the embodied subjectivity of the practising scholar, in this case myself: whom I call RyyA. Bread©.

2. To offer an abbreviated insight into the kinds of performative 'play' at work within my research and/of (identity) textual production.

Colour coordinates: the hue, what, where, when and why of subject specificity

Colour is used within my thesis as a navigating system to locate the coordinates of subjectivity in relation to the research process. Through the process of defining the embodied identity text(s) of RyyA. Bread©, the colour-coding schema began to emerge as a way of mapping and marking subject specificity. With this said, the colour-coding schema is most accurately described as a process of *colour coordination*, although both terms are used here interchangeably.

How *subjectivity* is framed within my project is crucial to an appreciation of the methodological function of this colour-coding schema. In a departure from Humanist constructions of a fixed, transparent Subject, *subjectivity* is understood within my work as embodied, fluid, shifting, multiple and performative. Moreover, the process of defining subjectivity is, indeed, a performative act of becoming a 'Subject'.

My whole thesis pivots around the identity text(s) of RyyA. Bread©, positioned as the *subject, object* and *author* of investigation. At the same time, the work is focused on (re)defining the term(s) [of] 'subjectivity' and critically developing a 'self'-referential methodology. Thus my strategy is to use (my)'self' as a case study for researching the interrelations of language, materiality and image within a mutually informed process of *reading* and *enacting* textual production(s). This approach was initiated at the outset of my recently completed doctoral research project in order to implicate the subject in the object and reveal a relation of fluid simultaneity that refuses crass binaries, such as mind/body and practice/theory.

Colour-coding schema
In shedding light on the subject of colour-coordination, the first thing to say is that my 'schema' is neither fixed nor finite. One of its defining features is that it remains in a continual state of development and transmutation. Secondly, the schema does not just refer to one 'code', nor is a particular colour limited in the number of potential referents it can signify at any one time. Thus, following on from this, the colour-coding schema has evolved over time in a 'collage'-like fashion across the different contexts, colours and content that it represents. Finally, the significance of the colour-coding schema has emerged slowly throughout the research process and therefore it is marked by its shifting position within the overall thesis. In brief, the colour-coding schema is understood as an indefinite, shifting, multi-layered and flexible framework that is consistent with, and bound up in, my reading of subjectivity.

Colour
My departing premise is that colour, like other signifiers, only 'matters' when it is in-*corporated* into subjective significance. Following on from this, my engagement with colour-(coding) has not been concerned with pre-existing discourses of 'colour theory', as it is conventionally understood in aesthetic or scientific terms. Instead, my use of colour is positioned within a broader concern for '(de/re/en)coding' with regard to identifying and representing subjectivity.

Subject specific 'significance'
A primary objective of my research has been to establish a set of criteria regarding 'significance' that could be applied to the process of framing subjectivity in an embodied way. This criteria is predicated on what I call *subject specificity*. My working understanding of the term is bound up with an individual's interpretation of their personal 'self', with regard to (auto)histories and circumstances; including (but not limited to) perceptions of physicality and sexuality. In other words, subject specificity is concerned with how the proverbial 'I' makes meaning out of lived experiences.

This article, about the significance of colour in my praxis, was written with the accompanied photographs (fig. 2-8) specifically intended as *colour images*.

Subjectivity with [a] 'difference'

My project is framed as a feminist project and uses the histories and ideologies of feminism(s) to locate my own interdisciplinary approach to research. In my formulation of the term subject specificity, I argue that 'difference', sexual and otherwise, both affects and effects the ways in which narratives of subjectivity and agency are constructed - individually and culturally. Classic psychoanalytic definitions of subjectivity, and post-structuralist understandings of the 'author function', are therefore critically explored within my research and given a socio-historical context from my position as a woman; engaged with questions of ontology, epistemology and aesthetics through a specific visual-material scholarly praxis.

A praxis prism

Subject specificity refers to both the embodied subject of the practitioner *and* subjects of study, within corresponding frameworks of multiplicity. These frameworks of multiplicity are mapped through colour-coding to locate a/the subject's position(s), or coordinates, within a particular context and activate a series of self-referential narratives.

The construction of such self-referential narratives corresponds with an understanding of subjectivity, of where 'I' begins and what the boundaries of my imaginary anatomy are in the context of scholarly research. My working definition of subjectivity is a departure from linear notions of progression such as, 'beginnings' and/or 'endings'. Everything that I am, everything that I experience(ed) and embody, I carry into my praxis and, according to my own methodology, it is all a contributing factor to my thesis.

Therefore, rather than 'begin' representing and inscribing embodiment, I have sought strategies of intervention into the processes of performativity that are already in motion. The colour-coding schema has emerged from such activities within my praxis.

The clues for how to proceed have been found in the slippage and excess of my subjectivity within and beyond the context of academic research. What events have led me to where I am at any particular moment? What activities am I performing at any given time? When I am not working on a specific research task, I am elsewhere engaged in some form of activity. What is the significance of this engagement to my subjectivity as it is defined within my praxis? In adopting this line of questioning as a way forward, the findings of my research have (always) already 'begun'. Thus my project becomes one of identification and articulation in order to incorporate embodied experiences into understanding; and exhibit such understandings through linguistic and visual-material textual production within a scholarly context.

Subject positions

Subject positions are identified and articulated through colour coordination. This process is an example of performative 'play' at work within my research. The following series of photographs (below) represent the working colour-coding schema of my doctoral thesis.[2] More will be said in a moment about the role of photography in my praxis. For the moment, however, I would like to focus on the significance of the subject positions with regard to colour coordination.

The colour coordinates correspond with the positions taken up by the 'subject (in-the-making)' RyyA. Bread©, during the course of the research period. The potential number of these positions is indefinite, and they are determined (in part) by context. These particular subject positions have been identified as significant to the research context of my specific praxis. The boundaries of these positions are not fixed, as there are overlaps and shifting markers. The first four colour coordinates are classified as *transient* positions, while the last four have a more clearly defined 'character'. These *identified character subject positions* were established before the transient positions were, even though they are listed afterwards in this particular presentation. Through an attempt to describe the relationships between the four identified character subject positions, the transient positions were introduced in these colourful subject specific terms. It is partially because of this chronological development that I read the transient subject positions as shadow positions, whose functions are implicit within the performative enactment of identity textual production.

Transient subject positions (see page 41)

* 'White' signifies the material *process* of embodied engagement within the praxis.
* 'Orange' signifies entrance into language through the *articulation* of the process.
* '(Jade) Green' (bottom left) and '(dark) purple' (bottom right) signify two distinct personas within my construct of the *Imaginary Other(s)*: the *Phantom Lover* and the *Imaginary M/Other* respectively.

Identified character subject positions (see page 42)

* 'Blue' signifies the daily negotiations between embodied experiences and pre-existing social constructions of *A/The Woman*, with respect to both sexual difference and subjective specificity.
* '(Lime) Green' signifies my occupation as what I call the *Professional Student*; this refers to both the protocol and academic context of the project as a doctoral thesis.
* 'Purple' signifies the artistic practices of the praxis with respect to the embodiment of the traditional notion of *A/The Artist* through a process of interrogation and redefinition.
* 'Magenta' signifies the *Scholarly Exhibitionist*. This is the position I posit to supersede the 'Artist' and more accurately reflect my locations within the praxis.

Colour coordination is a private performative process of mapping subject specific significance through a range of exercises, so as 1) to identify the ways in which I construct narratives of 'self'; and 2) to position my 'self' in relation to the people, places and things in my surrounding environment(s). It is not necessarily important that the auto-historical details or subject specific narratives that inform my work are made explicit for a reader. What is significant is the ways in which such mappings are per-formed and ultimately how they have in-formed the thesis as a whole, in order for it to con-form to a specific scholarly degree academic research. In keeping with this, I will refrain from detailing the personal significance attached to each colour used in my colour 'code' above. Instead I will continue to unpick how the colour-code has evolved by exploring the particular example of the colour 'white' in a bit more detail.

Figure 1 RyyA. Bread©: White – Process, *2000, 35mm colour slide.*

Figure 2 RyyA. Bread©: Orange – ARTiculation, *2000, 35mm colour slide.*

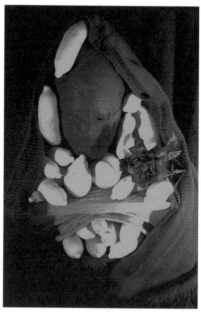

Figure 3 RyyA. Bread©: Jade Green – The Phantom Lover, *2000, 35mm colour slide.*

Figure 4 RyyA. Bread©: Dark Purple – Imaginary m/Other, *2000, 35mm colour slide.*

RyyA. Bread©

Figure 5 RyyA. Bread©: Blue – A/The Woman, *2000, 35mm colour slide.*

Figure 6 RyyA. Bread©: Purple – A/The Artist, *2000, 35mm colour slide.*

Figure 7 RyyA. Bread©: Purple – A/The Artist, *2000, 35mm colour slide.*

Figure 8 RyyA. Bread©: Magenta – The Scholarly Exhibitionist, *2000, 35mm colour slide.*

'Hue' am I?...

The [White-] Process of Identification

The first image presented in this series of photographs, 'White-process', depicts a still life installation of the materials used in my 'plaster coating exercise': one of the primary studio activities of *METHODOLOGICAL EMBODIMENTS*. The plaster coating exercise explores the translation of *autobiography* from a literary genre to a visual-material medium. The focus of this particular research exercise is on what can be performed and produced working alone in the studio and using my own body as the basis for subject specific representation.

The plaster coatings are constructed through a process of saturating muslin with wet plaster and covering those sections of my body that I can reach. Through the intimate encounter between the wet muslin and my body, a thin plaster/cloth skin dries over my form and hardens into an object in its own right. This is followed by a separation period in which my body is removed from within the plaster coating. By 'writing the body' in this way, my embodied presence is inscribed within, and shapes, the form of the plaster coatings. My body, which has been 'written' by auto-historical circumstances and embodied experiences prior to its material contact with the plaster coatings, is also further informed through these performative (life) experiences.

In the image of 'White-process', materials are used to refer to the plaster coatings; an exercise that takes materiality as a departure point into self-referential narratives. The materials of the plaster coating process are predominantly 'white': the plaster in raw powder form, the muslin before it is dipped in the wet plaster, the garment worn between plaster coatings, and the final plaster coatings of my body. Insofar as my body is an intrinsic material used in the making of the coatings, my 'white' skin colour is also a significant inclusion in this list with regard to subject specificity and narrative constructions of identity.

My photography practice is also implicated in 'White-process', as the mode of textual production. Photography is a visual-material practice used within my praxis to record private performances such as the plaster coating exercise and the colour coordination still-life installations. The photographic activity, however, is also a performance itself and it represents a playful exploration between personal narratives, objects of association and visual textual production.

The departure point of my photography practice enters into the discourse of self-referential narratives from a different place than the plaster coating exercise. Rather than the materiality of embodiment and praxis, image and imaginary processes of identification and projection lead the photographic practice. One of the roles of my photography practice is to identify and entertain the associative investments that I have with personal possessions. One way that this task is performed is through the construction and photographic recording of still-life installations such as those pertaining to my colour-coding scheme. While my relationship to such objects may initially be far removed from the research context, by 'putting them in the picture', as Jo Spence (1986) would say, they become implicated in my methodological process. By being positioned in this way, they then have the potential to be followed through and picked up by other overlapping narrative constructions pertaining to *METHODOLOGICAL EMBODIMENTS*.

The photography formats that I use most often are 35mm colour slide film or digital still image capturing. I do not develop my own film. By the same token, my concern with creating installations and performative moments of play has priority over lighting and other technical concerns. To this end, my photography practice

RyyA. Bread©

can be seen as a sketching tool for exploring ideas in a fluid stage of conception, rather than producing a thoroughly distilled (identity) text.

The significance of 'colour' within my (subject specific) mapping of meaning is extracted from the sites and sights of my personal possessions and domestic environments: in particular articles of clothing and food. These same objects are used in the photographic still-life installations to signify particular activities, people and events that define my life: past, present and future. Over time, layers of images and associations with the objects are identified through my photography exercises and 'framed' in relation to the other elements of my praxis. Through this process, colour coordination provides a language in which to dress the body of work.

Through the calling out of RyyA. Bread© in this way, subject specificity materializes and becomes visible. This strategy is intended to enter the Symbolic Order through senses and sensibilities that are informed by image and materiality and cannot be directly translated into or represented exclusively by verbal (script) modes of representation. Thus the subject positions signalled through the photographs become representative and representatives of an embodied methodology that cannot be defined simply with words.

The overlapping of themes is an essential aspect of the interplay, how themes overlap and simultaneously remain distinct to a respective medium is part of the inquiry. As a performative structural function, colour coordination allows my identity text(s) as RyyA. Bread© to 'be' in more than one place at the same time and to 'have' the means to illuminate and refract the light that defines my praxis prism.

References:

Burke, S. (1992), *The Death & Return of the Author: Criticism and Subjectivity in Barthes, Foucault and Derrida*, Edinburgh: Edinburgh University Press, p. 27

Butler, J. (1990), *Gender Trouble: Feminism and the Subversion of Identity*. New York and London: Routledge.

Lichtenburg Ettinger, B. (1996), 'The With-In-Visible-Screen', in de Zegher, M.C. (ed.) (1996), *Inside The Visible: An Elliptical Traverse of 20th Century Art in, of, and from the Feminine*, Cambridge, Mass.: MIT Press, pp. 89-113 (Introduction by Pollock, G, pp. 89-92).

Spence, J. (1986), *Putting Myself in the Picture: A Political, Personal and Photographic Autobiography*, London: Camden Press.

Categories in action: Sartre and the theory-practice debate

Clive Cazeaux

Abstract

This paper addresses the topic of creative practice research degrees by looking at the role concepts play in the creation and appreciation of art. The nature of the relationship between conceptual judgement on the one hand and aesthetic experience on the other has been a central topic for discussion throughout the history of Western philosophy. Unfortunately, the greater part of that history has given us arguments which try to wedge the two apart. However, the phenomenological tradition within recent continental philosophy sets out to remove the opposition between the conceptual and the aesthetic. Two aspects of phenomenology are important here: 1) its interest in writing, and 2) its emphasis on our condition as beings immersed in and actively engaged with the world, as opposed to being detached observers of it. The two come together in the claim that the concept - any concept - is not something which confines or reduces experience but an 'action' through which the speaker brings to light new aesthetic possibilities. By tracing these points through the writings of Kant, Nietzsche and Sartre, I show how the descriptions we employ in aesthetic judgement a) can stand alongside the physical gestures of the artist as 'constructive interventions' in the development of an artwork, and b) can bring new perspectives to bear on the theoretical framework employed by the practitioner in their research.

Categories in action: Sartre and the theory-practice debate

1 Examples of the appeal to metaphysics, to a realm beyond our own, made in order to account for art's departure from representation, can be found in the following: Hermann Bahr, *Expressionism*, trans. R.T. Gribble, London: Frank Henderson, 1920; André Breton, 'Surrealism and Painting', *Art in Theory 1900-1990*, eds. Charles Harrison and Paul Wood, Oxford: Blackwell, 1992, pp. 440-46; Barbara Hepworth, 'Sculpture', *Art in Theory 1900-1990, op. cit.*, pp.

The relationship between art theory and art practice continues to be the subject of much debate. There are several reasons for this, all of them interconnected. Firstly, the growth of interest in art and design as subjects of academic research, undertaken by both staff and graduate students within university art departments, has led to questions regarding the status of art as knowledge, for example, whether art can be quantified as a form of knowledge or whether it should have to be quantified as such. Secondly, and following on from the first point, many of the concepts of art that have been bequeathed to us by modernism do not encourage integration between theory and practice. Whether it is a sustained commitment to the modernist dictum of art for art's sake or adherence to the metaphysical doctrines that went hand in hand with modernism's departure from representation, modern art has often claimed for itself a purity or spontaneity that places it or its essence beyond classification, beyond words.[1] This debate ultimately falls back on a third arena: the history of the theory of knowledge. The greater part of that history gives us arguments which try to wedge conceptual judgement and aesthetic experience apart. I am thinking here primarily of the epistemologies of Plato and Descartes, both of which argue to the effect that rational knowledge is of a wholly distinct order from sensory experience. And even when there are subsequent

JVAP 2 (1&2) 44–56 ©Intellect Ltd 2002

attempts to reconcile these two orders, by Hume and Kant for example, these are shown to be problematic.

Given the way in which the theory-practice question ultimately unfolds itself to become questions about how we theorize knowledge or *kinds* of knowledge, it is understandable why discussion continues with such vigour. The amount of history behind the debate might prompt one to think that any intervention at this stage is futile; it must surely be impossible to resist or redirect the millennia-old patterns of thought which lead us to separate reason from sensation. However, what I propose to do in this paper is a) show how recent developments within continental aesthetics challenge the opposition between the conceptual and the aesthetic, and b) show how this challenge has implications for the way we perceive the relationship between theory and practice in art and design research degrees.

The work being done in continental aesthetics represents a radical rethinking of the position of the self in the world, and the way in which the self acts in and gains knowledge of the world. The existentialism of Jean-Paul Sartre is particularly relevant to the theory-practice debate, I maintain, in as much as he translates a theory of being into a theory of action, where the making of art and the description of aesthetic experience are seen as two of the principal kinds of action through which the self creates meaning in the world. One consequence of this, as far as we are concerned, is that the theoretical perspectives adopted by the artist can be seen to stand alongside the physical gestures made by the artist in the studio as 'constructive interventions' in the development of an artwork. Against this backdrop, the word or concept, far from being something which confines or is antithetical to experience (as it is represented in Platonic and Cartesian epistemologies), in fact emerges as an 'action' through which the artist-as-researcher brings new aesthetic possibilities to light.

Is creative practice research different from the kinds of research normally conducted for the Ph.D.? This question illustrates quite clearly how our immediate interest in the status of art and design research rests upon larger questions about the nature of knowledge. Further confirmation of this (if it were needed) is the fact that the theory-practice distinction belongs to a series of distinctions in the history of epistemology, all of which claim a difference and imply a value according to the origin or location of knowledge. These distinctions include:

conceptual – aesthetic
theory – practice
verbal – visual
mental – physical
objective – subjective

In all of the above, it is usually the case that the left-hand term is regarded as the source of knowledge or the more direct route to it, whereas the right-hand term is seen as that which *is incidental to* or which *has to be overcome* in the production of knowledge. Understandably, people working in art and design education would want to contest this weighting against the aesthetic side of the distinction. In fact, much of the debate around what qualifies as research for a Ph.D. in art or design, I suggest, is devoted to grappling with the question of how the aesthetic should stand in relation to the conceptual in order for it to be able to comply with the requirements set for verbal, objective knowledge, as demonstrated, for example, by

374-77; Wassily Kandinsky, *Concerning the Spiritual in Art*, trans. M.T.H. Sadler, New York: Dover, 1977; Gerhard Richter as quoted in Bernice Rose, *Allegories of Modernism: Contemporary Drawing*, New York: Museum of Modern Art, 1992, p. 44.

2 Plato, *The Republic*, trans. Desmond Lee, London: Penguin, 1987, 502c-521b.

3 René Descartes, 'Second Meditation', *Discourse on Method and the Meditations*, trans. F.E. Sutcliffe, Harmondsworth: Penguin, 1968, pp. 102-12.

4 Aristotle, *Prior Analytics*, trans. P.T. Geach, in *A New Aristotle Reader*, ed. J.L. Ackrill, Oxford: Clarendon, 1987, 24b, p. 25, emphasis added.

5 Arthur Schopenhauer, *The World as Will and Representation*, vol. 2, trans. E.F.J. Payne, New York: Dover, 1969, p. 74.

a university's Ph.D. regulations. Inevitably, these discussions look for ways in which the aesthetic can borrow or import some aspects from the conceptual, such as the introduction of research methodologies from other subject areas, the requirement of a substantial theoretical component, and the prediction of an outcome.

When one encounters distinctions of the type given above, there is a tendency to view them as oppositional distinctions, that is, distinctions where one side is antithetical or diametrically opposed to the other. Once again, the history of epistemology has to take some of the blame for this. Plato pictures ideas and physical reality as belonging to two separate worlds,[2] while Descartes presents concepts as being clear and constant in contrast to the muddy and organic flux of our bodily, material world.[3] However, the metaphor which is arguably the most virulent in making us think of these terms as opposites is Aristotle's notion of the concept as a container. As part of his exposition of syllogistic logic in *Prior Analytics*, Aristotle explains the process whereby all instances of a particular kind of object can be described as having the same property, for example, 'all cats have four legs'. 'That one term should be included *in another, as in a whole*', Aristotle writes, 'is the same as for the other to be predicated of all the first'.[4] Thus, in my example, to predicate 'having four legs' of all cats is the same as thinking of all cats being *inside* the category of 'having four legs'. The category is pictured as a container, something which embraces all the possible objects which might display the property in question. This metaphor was consolidated in 1880 by the English logician John Venn who introduced the convention of representing concepts as circles in order to allow syllogistic arguments to be represented as diagrams (known as Venn diagrams).

While this way of thinking about concepts and the relation they have to what is conceptualized, i.e. what goes inside them, is useful in some contexts, it nevertheless has the negative consequence of presenting the relation between concept and content as a strict binary division: concepts as containers are quite distinct from the things that go inside them. One version of this view, in an idiom which is closer to home, is that concepts or words are inadequate compared to experience. The thinking here is that concepts, because of their generality, because they have to contain an indefinite number of similar situations, cannot possibly exhibit the vivacity or immediacy of the individual thing or moment. Schopenhauer makes this observation in *The World as Will and Representation*: 'Books do not take the place of experience', he writes, 'because concepts always remain universal, and do not reach down to the particular; yet it is precisely the particular that has to be dealt with in life'.[5] Note how the conflicting interests of objectivity and subjectivity (one of the contrasting pairs which fall under the conceptual-aesthetic distinction, if we recall) are manifest in this example. As far as objective knowledge is concerned, generality or universality is to be encouraged, since it is a measure of the applicability of one's terms, whereas for subjective experience, generality represents a flattening out of all that is present in the moment.

Perceiving the conceptual and the aesthetic in such a way that it is always possible to see one as utterly separate from and independent of the other, as in the case of a container and the items which might happen to go into it, can only perpetuate the situation whereby the theory and practice of art are seen as unwilling partners. Ultimately, such separationism can do little to demonstrate the epistemic value of creative practice research, for the simple reason that 'objectivity', on this understanding, is antithetical to art by definition. Interestingly enough, Schopenhauer's observation occurs in the context of an argument which is trying to

Clive Cazeaux

establish the importance of aesthetic experience *over* rational judgement. Unfortunately, however, Schopenhauer's argument leaves the fundamental opposition between the conceptual and the aesthetic intact. He simply elevates one side at the expense of the other, moving to one extreme in order to compensate for a tradition which has always privileged its opposite.

How then are we to avoid this impasse? Trying to overcome the opposition by collapsing the distinctions is not the answer because it is quite plain that each distinction marks an important difference, and it is important to retain these differences: words are not the same as images, the conceptual is not the same as the aesthetic, and theory is not the same as practice. However, seeing them as diametrically opposed is only one way of regarding the contrasts. One of the most potentially fruitful lines of investigation, I think, is to look for other ways of understanding the differences at work in the above distinctions. While the majority of the images and arguments from the history of epistemology encourage us to view the conceptual and the aesthetic as opposites, recent developments in continental aesthetics have begun to challenge this opposition. Instead of regarding concepts as containers, theories are on offer in the continental tradition which represent the concept as that which, in relation to experience, sculpts, gives shape, offers purchase, illuminates, differentiates, ruptures, ripples, or contours.[6]

These notions can be plotted in many ways throughout recent continental thought but, I suggest, they all have their origin in Kant's critical philosophy, i.e. they are all ultimately extensions of or responses to his thinking. One of the most direct routes, certainly for our concern, is a line from Kant, through Nietzsche, to Sartre. Kant and Nietzsche might seem unusual partners - Kant, an eighteenth-century Enlightenment thinker, and Nietzsche, a nineteenth-century nihilist - but, as I shall demonstrate, continuity exists between them on account of their theorization of conceptuality.

The central premise of Kant's epistemology is that the consciousness of the experiencing subject and the organization of external reality exist in a reciprocal relationship. That is to say, in order for experience to take place, for there to be any experience at all, there must be something *which has the experience* - the subject - and something *which that experience is experience of* - the object. What is novel about Kant's thinking here is that subject and object, rather than being theorized as separate or isolated entities, are seen as positions defined in relation to one another, opposite ends of the unified spectrum of experience, one side shading into the other. The relevance of this theory to our study is that it is concepts within the mind of the subject, for Kant, which confer the unity necessary for intelligible, organized experience to occur. In the 'transcendental deduction', the principal argument of the *Critique of Pure Reason*, Kant argues that both identity of the self and the determination of objects within intuition (*Anschauung*, Kant's term for the world as it appears to us) derive from the unity conferred by concepts:

> The original and necessary consciousness of the identity of the self is thus at
> the same time a consciousness of an equally necessary unity of the synthesis of
> all appearances according to concepts, that is, according to rules, which not
> only make them necessarily reproducible but also in so doing determine an
> object for their intuition, that is, the concept of something wherein they are
> necessarily connected.[7]

6 These descriptions of the concept, and the way I draw them out from Sartre's philosophy, are extensions of the theme I discuss in my article 'Theorizing Theory and Practice', *Point: Art and Design Research Journal*, 7, 1999, pp. 26-31. In this paper, I examine the concept of truth as *aletheia* in Kantian epistemology and the philosophy of science. In contrast to the conventional notion of truth as correspondence to reality, *aletheia* refers to the perceptual processes which first bring a reality into being. In this regard, *aletheia* might be likened to photosynthesis: perception draws an object into existence in the same way that the sun draws a plant from the soil. It is the notion of making something stand out or up from a surface, something that makes a difference against an otherwise uniform terrain, that I am developing in relation to Sartre.

7 Immanuel Kant, *Critique of Pure Reason*, trans. Norman Kemp Smith, London: Macmillan, 1990, A108, pp. 136-37.

8 Friedrich Nietzsche, 'On Truth and Lie in an Extra-Moral Sense', *The Continental Aesthetics Reader*, ed. Clive Cazeaux, London: Routledge, 2000, p. 55, emphases added.

Thus the concept, as Kant understands it, is that element within the subject's cognitive apparatus which reaches out into the world and carves it into a shape which can then go on to play a recognizable and therefore a stabilizing role in the subject's experience of the world. In this way, continuous, unified experience *for the subject* and perception of solid, stable objects *in an external reality* are both brought into being.

Nietzsche extends this particular line of Kantianism by arguing for the creativity of concept-formation. In putting forward this view, Nietzsche is challenging the notion of the concept as an order-giving principle, where the order in question is held to derive from an external, i.e. metaphysical, source. The sources which he typically has in mind are religious doctrine, Plato's concept of the Forms, and the theologically informed rationalism of Descartes. Against these standpoints, Nietzsche argues that perception is a transformative process, and that all concepts are originally metaphors, created as a part of this process. The images which make up our vision, the sounds which make up our hearing, the textures which make up our touch, etc., are not copies or impressions of the objects which give rise to them, but phenomena that are created as a result of the transformational relationship which our faculties have with the world. As he observes in his essay 'On Truth and Lie in an Extra-Moral Sense',

> To begin with, a nerve stimulus is transferred into an image: first metaphor. The image, in turn, is imitated in sound: second metaphor. And each time there is a complete overleaping of one sphere, right into the middle of an entirely new and different one. One can imagine a man who is totally deaf and has never had a sensation of sound and music. Perhaps such a person will gaze with astonishment at Chladni's sound figures; perhaps he will discover their causes in the vibrations of the string and will now swear that he must know what men mean by 'sound'. *It is this way with all of us concerning language:* we believe that we know something about the things themselves when we speak of trees, colours, snow, and flowers; and yet we possess nothing but metaphors for things - *metaphors which correspond in no way to the original entities.*[8]

Chladni's sound figures are the patterns and shapes created by directing the vibrations from a plucked string into a bed of sand, as demonstrated by the nineteenth-century physicist Ernst Chladni. What they show for Nietzsche is that the phenomenon we call sound is simply a manifestation of the way in which our faculties interpret reality. If, as Nietzsche claims, all perception is a process of metaphorical transference, then a figure in sand is just as valid and appropriate a rendition of that part of the world we call 'sound' as sound is itself. On this account, a concept is not a container which groups together all the entities in the world which correspond to it, but that point in the perceptual process where our faculties, through the various metaphorical transformations they perform, give some definite and recognizable shape to what would otherwise be an indifferent and incohate reality.

The importance which these arguments from Kant and Nietzsche have for Sartre's existentialism cannot be overestimated. They prepare the ground for Sartre in two respects. Firstly, Kant's and Nietzsche's rejection of the view that a concept is a distinct or isolatable unity representing an essence or a metaphysical given lends support to Sartre's repudiation of the substantive self. Whereas Platonic and

Cartesian epistemologies assert that human beings have their innermost nature, including their moral being, determined in advance of experience by metaphysical essences (with Plato) or pure rationality (with Descartes), existentialism declares that the individual constructs themselves through action *in the absence of* an abiding, determinative moral agency. Sartre rejects outright the thesis that we are defined and motivated by a priori concepts or essences: 'the act is everything. Behind the act there is neither potency nor "hexis" nor virtue'.[9] Rather, it is only through active transformation of or engagement with the world, Sartre avows, that people and things acquire meanings. I explain this in more detail below.

Secondly, the ways in which meaning and identity can be created through action are devised by Sartre as an extension of the theories of conceptuality proposed by Kant and Nietzsche. If all previous conceptions of truth, i.e. those which assign truth a metaphysical or purely rational origin, are rejected, then one is left with the situation where truth *has to be made*. Or, to make the same point from another perspective, Kant and Nietzsche provide us with theories in which the borders between subjectivity and objectivity are not so clearly drawn. As a result, a closer examination of the role played by concepts in experience is necessary in order to understand more fully the processes through which the subject carves up the world into a meaningful set of objects and experiences, including the experience of self.

Sartre's work along these lines casts light upon the theory-practice debate in as much as he devises what (I suggest) might be called a 'topography of action'. He studies how an action makes a difference to a situation in such a way that that difference becomes an object of attention, something which represents a moment of distinction in what would otherwise be a continuous, undifferentiated flow of experience. This view of action is topographical in the sense that acting, carrying out a gesture, making an impression on the world are events which rise above or drop below the flat line of inactivity. It is in terms of these ripples, bumps, crevices, and impressions, Sartre argues, that we must begin to construct our notions of meaning and personal identity.

We can see this in relation to Sartre's configuration of the self. I shall go into some detail as Sartre's thinking here is central to the point I want to make in relation to art theory and practice. The subject, following Kant and Nietzsche, rather than being a distinct, self-contained entity, is shown to be something so intimately intertwined with the world that any clear-cut division is problematic; this is a self that is very much *in the world*. Sartre's response to this is to theorize the self as a 'gap' in the world. What is unique to consciousness, Sartre argues, is that it is the location of the perception of absence: it is only in consciousness that the impression of something *not being the case* can take place, for example, expecting to find thirty pounds in my wallet but finding only twenty, or waiting in a café for a friend who never turns up. As he states:

> Every question in essence posits the possibility of a negative reply. In a question
> we question a being about its being or its way of being. This way of being or
> this being is veiled; there always remains the possibility that it may unveil itself
> as a Nothingness. But from the very fact that we presume that an Existent can
> always be revealed as *nothing*, every question supposes that we realize a
> nihilating withdrawal in relation to the given, which becomes a simple
> presentation, fluctuating between being and Nothingness.

9

10 ibid,
11 ibi
12

'. a magica.
impulse.

. 23.

., p. 27.

ibid., pp. 28-29.

It is essential therefore that the questioner has the permanent possibility of dissociating himself from the causal series which constitutes being and which can produce only being.[10]

It is the possibility of negation which disengages consciousness from the brute causal order of the world; 'this cleavage is precisely nothingness'.[11] A cleavage divides the present of consciousness from all its past, 'not as a phenomenon which it experiences, [but] rather as a structure of consciousness which it is'.[12] This rupture in the causal order of the world *is* the structure of consciousness for Sartre. The perception of absence or negation creates a gap in experience, and it is because of this rupture or interval that the subject is able to become aware of itself standing before a world. It also means that there can never be a moment when consciousness is identical with an abiding, substantive self which can influence or determine its actions; rather, consciousness only exists in the world as a gap or a nothingness between things.

This would seem to paint a bleak picture of our situation, but this is only because our *conventional* notion of subjectivity is being repudiated here. By defining subjectivity as a nothingness, Sartre is making the point that the self is constructed through its engagement with the world, by dealing with whatever is brought before it as a bump or a rupture in the field of experience. In this regard, Sartre's writing might be described as a philosophy of confrontation, not in an antagonistic or hostile sense but in the sense that we are made to reflect upon how we might face up to a situation and all its implications. The full force of the confrontation perhaps only becomes apparent when it is recognized that this reflection has to occur in the absence of the concept of a 'true' self, the concept which might otherwise reject certain possibilities on the grounds that we are a *particular kind of person*, inclined to act in certain ways.

What this topography of action brings to the theory-practice debate is a way of thinking which allows art theory and art practice to stand alongside each other as mutually supportive 'interventions' in the development of an artwork. On this account, both theory and practice can be understood as gestures which *make a difference*, make something stand out, rise above or drop below an otherwise undifferentiated field of experience. While we are probably accustomed to thinking of art practice as a form of action, it needs to be borne in mind that activity, i.e. activity in general, is being viewed here from a particular, existentialist perspective. With Sartre, we are theorizing the action as an event, a moment, a rupture, something which makes a difference where there was previously no difference at all, and which thereby allows the subject to orient itself in terms of the objects it encounters. Approaching the art-making process in these terms requires us to think about the way in which the work develops as a series of ruptures or saliences, for example, the effect of a brushstroke on an area of canvas, the prominence of a particular object in the viewfinder, the accentuation of certain qualities on a ceramic surface, the masking of those elements in a location which might interfere with a site-specific work.

In actual fact, this point is not terribly new. It is simply a means of talking about the focus of the artist's attention, but with the recognition that 'focus' belongs to our family of topographical terms denoting the concentration of attention, the *bringing-together to a point*. However, the location of focus is particularly important for the artist-as-researcher, for enrolment on a programme of research inevitably involves the statement of aims, objectives, and methodologies, i.e. a description of

Clive Cazeaux

the particular aspects of art which are to be the subject of research, and an account of why these aspects are being focused upon.

The greater amount of work to be done, it would seem, lies with the question of how the theorization of art is accommodated within Sartre's topography of action, especially when writing about art is, in comparison to making the stuff, such a sedate occupation. Also, the form of prose itself conceals the *activity* of writing: a linear flow of sentences and paragraphs, arguments and conclusions, cannot reflect or display the mental effort and torment which wrought them into being. However, as I indicate above, when action is discussed in a Sartrean context, we cannot simply fall back on the conventional notion of action as physical bodies moving in space. Instead, we are now considering it as the creation of a rupture or cleavage in the flow of experience.

Writing holds a position of special significance in Sartre's philosophy precisely because it is one of the principal ways of rupturing or interrupting experience. And it is able to do this for the same reason that many people (including Schopenhauer) see it as being removed from life: writing involves the application of concepts to experience, of generalities to particularities. The distinction between generality and particularity is crucial, Sartre thinks, because it introduces a gap between consciousness and experience. He explores this dimension of writing at length in his novel *Nausea*. The book is a study of the non-identity between words and experience. The central character, Antoine Roquentin, is living in Bouville and trying to write a biography of the late-eighteenth-century political activist Monsieur de Rollebon. However, he gives up the project when the minutiae of his own life encroach on him with ever increasing detail and sublimity, and convince him of the futility of trying to represent experience. The written word, it seems to Roquentin, will always distance you from experience, will never allow you to be identical with the present. The novel's first page outlines the diarist's dilemma:

> The best thing would be to write down everything that happens from day to day. To keep a diary in order to understand. To neglect no nuances or little details, even if they seem unimportant, and above all to classify them. I must say how I see this table, the street, people, my packet of tobacco, since *these* are the things which have changed. I must fix the exact extent and nature of this change.
>
> For example, there is a cardboard box which contains my bottle of ink. I ought to try to say how I saw it *before* and how I —— it now. Well, it's a parallelepiped rectangle standing out against - that's silly, there's nothing I can say about it. That's what I must avoid: I mustn't put strangeness where there's nothing. I think that is the danger of keeping a diary: you exaggerate everything, you are on the look-out, and you continually search the truth. On the other hand, it is certain that from one moment to the next - and precisely in connexion with this box or any other object - I may recapture this impression of the day before yesterday. I must always be prepared, or else it might slip through my fingers again. I must never —— anything but note down carefully and in the greatest detail everything that happens.[13]

The ellipses - 'how I —— it now' and 'I must never —— anything' - are acknowledged in the text with the respective footnotes: 'A word is missing here' and 'A word has been crossed out here (possibly "force" or "forge"), and another word has been

13 Jean-Paul Sartre, *Nausea*, trans. Robert Baldick, London: Penguin, 1963, p. 9.

14 Sartre, *Being and Nothingness*, op. cit., p. xli.

15 *ibid.*, p. xxxvii.

16 Sartre, *Nausea*, op. cit., p. 186.

17 *ibid.*, pp. 61-63.

18 Martin Heidegger, *Being and Time*, trans. John Macquarrie and Edward Robinson, Oxford: Blackwell, 1962, nn. 15-16, pp. 95-107.

written above it which is illegible'. By leaving these gaps, Sartre makes it apparent from the start that language introduces a specificity which is not present in experience. The crossings-out are important: 'force', an exertion of will or an impulse to change the state or position of an object; 'forge', on the one hand, to give shape to what was originally shapeless or, on the other, to copy, to fashion something which is inauthentic.

The task of verbal description, for Sartre, reflects the cognitive relationship between being-for-itself (*être-pour-soi*, human being) and being-in-itself (*être-en-soi*, the being of objects). Objects, Sartre asserts, exist in themselves; they belong to the in-itself. The being of objects is 'full positivity': 'an immanence which cannot realize itself, an affirmation which cannot affirm itself, an activity which cannot act, because it is glued to itself'.[14] This makes objects opaque for us. Objects resist us in the world, assert a counter-pressure against perception, because they never disclose themselves all at once. On this account, it is precisely because things are to some degree closed to us that we have consciousness at all; consciousness is the partial, sequential disclosedness of things. Experience is successive: a continuum in which aspects appear and disappear, in which appearances are revealed and then withdrawn. Impressions move on: the object is not present to me now in the exact same way it was a moment ago. If all impressions were present in one instance, Sartre comments, the objective 'would dissolve in the subjective'.[15] However, just as the appearance and disappearance of phenomena enable the perception of absence, so the application of general categories to particular experience puts experience at a distance, creates a phenomenological opening between writer and experience. As soon as Roquentin describes the bark of the tree-root as 'black', he feels 'the word subside, empty itself of its meaning with an extraordinary speed. Black? The root was not black, it was not the black there was on that piece of wood - it was ... something else'.[16] The perception that the generality of a word cannot capture the particularity of an object, that *something is missing*, thus appears, from Sartre's position, as one of the crevices in our topography of action and, therefore, as an episode that is vital to the construction of subjectivity and objectivity.

Because of the gap between universal and particular, description alters the situation. As Sartre observes, writing gives order and significance to something which is 'not yet there':

> When you are living, nothing happens. The settings change, people come in and go out, that's all. There are never any beginnings. Days are tacked on without rhyme or reason, it is an endless, monotonous addition ... But when you tell about life, everything changes; only it's a change nobody notices: the proof of that is that people talk about true stories. As if there could possibly be such things as true stories; events take place one way and we recount them the opposite way. You appear to begin at the beginning: 'It was a fine autumn evening in 1922. I was a solicitor's clerk at Marommes.' And in fact you have begun at the end.[17]

Sartre is building on Heidegger here, in particular, the distinction he draws in *Being and Time* between 'readiness-to-hand' (*Zuhandenheit*) and 'presence-at-hand' (*Vorhandenheit*).[18] The former denotes the state of busy, immersed occupation in which we deal with everyday activities, where objects are simply zones of interaction diffused into the greater backdrop of our routine intentions. For example, you walk

Clive Cazeaux

across the zebra crossing on your way to work but are not aware of the exact number of stripes. In contrast, 'presence-at-hand' refers to occasions when, for whatever reason, we are stopped in our tracks and what was formerly the mere furniture of existence stands out as a thing, *against* a background, whose nature suddenly becomes of detached perceptual or conceptual interest. This, Sartre observes, is what writing does. Imposing a subject-predicate structure on otherwise diffuse interaction breaks (in Heidegger's idiom) the 'referential totality' of equipment and elevates the thing so that it 'announces itself afresh'.[19]

A comment often made against the description of experience is that it introduces a specificity which was not present in the original experience; grammatical structure and conceptual boundaries impose a level of organization which is not in keeping with the lived moment. The sentence is a specific arrangement of two basic elements, a subject and a predicate, e.g. the sky is blue, in the face of a world that is otherwise indifferent and multifarious. From all that could be said at that moment, one selection, one slice across phenomena is made: the sky is blue. What had the character of a unique and particular experience is reduced or broken down into a set of general categories. In some sense, conceptualization does *shoe-horn* experience into categories which, in virtue of their generality, alter the shape of the experience, but it is wrong to be afraid of the metaphors of resistance and deformation which are implicit here. 'Deformation' is value-laden, and easily interpreted as an act of violence against experience by the concept. However, this sense arises solely because we have the misplaced ideal of a concept that should be identical to its object, that should fit or contain it perfectly. On the contrary, I assert, the sense of resistance which accompanies conceptualization should be embraced since it is precisely this resculpting of experience which, according to Sartre, grants language its active, salience-creating capacity.

Nausea can be regarded as the diary of someone coming to terms with the realization that writing does not capture experience but, instead, disrupts experience, announces the existence of things, gives experience shape and form. Towards the end of the novel, Roquentin realizes that the complete description of experience - when the word captures or contains the thing - is an impossibility and *it is the undecidability of description* which is 'the key to [his] Existence, the key to [his] Nausea'.[20] How should or could he describe the tree-root? 'snake or claw or root or vulture's talon', 'a suction-pump', its 'hard, compact sea-lion skin', its 'oily, horny, stubborn look'; 'knotty, inert, *nameless*'.[21] Similarly, when he looks at his hand spread out on the table, it seems to become first a 'crab', showing its 'under-belly', then a 'fish'; his fingers become 'paws', then 'claws'.[22]

What is on offer from Sartre then is a new way of understanding the relationship between concepts and experience. Instead of the conventional model of concept and experience being mutually exclusive terms where the former is held to contain the latter, the concept is presented by Sartre as a rupture or an interruption in experience, the consequence of which is that an aspect of reality is raised up before the individual as an object, as something which helps to define the subjectivity of the individual. This theory of language, and the existentialism of which it is a part, can be very useful in the context of creative practice research, I suggest, on two accounts. Firstly, rather than being regarded as separate and unrelated activities, theory and practice, from Sartre's perspective, become parallel or congruent processes on account of the fact that they both create salience or assign prominence; that is to say, they are both processes whereby new objects of attention

19 *ibid.*, nn. 16, pp. 105-07.

20 Sartre, *Nausea, op. cit.*, p. 185.

21 *ibid.*, pp. 185-86.

22 *ibid.*, pp. 143-44.

23 This, of course, is not to say that the *empirically verifiable* qualities in a work cannot become the subjects of *aesthetic* interest in the work. For example, an artist for whom the dimensions of painting are their main area of investigation will be working to produce paintings or related objects which allow the significance of this aspect to emerge, i.e. to become prominent, but - and this is the crucial point - on this account, it won't just be the measurements which are reflected upon but *the way in which the artworks point to or draw out the significance of their dimensions*. This will not be an empirically verifiable property but, instead, will be the subject of aesthetic judgement.

24 See David Hume, 'Of the Standard of Taste', *Selected Essays*, eds. Stephen Copley and Andrew Edgar, Oxford: Oxford University Press, 1993, pp. 133-53.

25 Immanuel Kant, *Critique of Judgement*, trans. Werner S. Pluhar, Indianapolis: Hacket, 1987. See, in particular, nn. 32-38, 44-46, 49, 56-57.

are brought before the viewer; it is just that the one does it through the application of words, while the other does it through the manipulation of art media.

Secondly, Sartre's theory of description, I maintain, can inform our understanding of the way in which theory and practice interact with one another. I can best develop this claim by anticipating an objection to my argument as it stands so far. It could be objected that I am moving from talk about description to talk about theory, as if the two were identical, when of course they are not. The theoretical component in creative practice research is much more than simply the description of the work carried out as part of that research. However, the description of an artwork is vital to the relationship between the studio practice which creates the work and the theoretical context in which that production takes place. This is because a work of art is always a work under interpretation, is always a work under aesthetic judgement.

Aesthetic judgement here appears in contradistinction to empirical judgement. To describe a work of art purely in terms of empirical judgements would be to list all those qualities about the work that are verifiable through observation and measurement, which are principally the materials used and the work's physical dimensions. While decisions about these are undeniably important for the artist/researcher, there is the question of how empirical qualities can have or acquire the significance which might make them subjects of theoretical enquiry; for empirical qualities themselves, on their own, are not the source of the meaning or significance of an artwork. Rather, this comes from the aesthetic judgements which are made about the work. For example, the size of a large-scale painting is significant not because its dimensions happen to be, say, 400 cm x 300 cm but because it has a particular *aesthetic* impact on the viewer, perhaps in terms of the perception of space or the human form or in relation to other large-scale media, such as advertising or film.[23] By 'aesthetic judgement', I don't just mean purely subjective statements of taste but also intend the term to cover all the interpretations and conceptual associations which are attached to the work, for example, the assessment of composition, the feeling or meaning evoked by the handling of form, and the way in which our perception of an object is defamiliarized by the work. My justification for this and, in fact, the basis of my approach in this paragraph, is Kant's aesthetic theory, especially as it is constructed in response to Hume's aesthetics. Following Hume's struggle to try and locate the value of art - is it in the eye of the beholder or a quality rooted in the constitution of the object itself?[24] - Kant transforms this undecidability into a condition of conceptual freeplay: in short, we are impressed by works of art (Kant argues) because, in an attempt to come to terms with them, i.e. to come to terms with them *conceptually*, we are prompted to reflect upon the categories through which we view the world at large.[25]

Thus the way we describe artworks, the judgements we make about them and the associations we bring to them are crucial for supplying the cognitive significance which can begin to be the subject of theoretical investigation. Trying to define the nature and scope of art theory is by no means a straightforward task but, for our purposes, in the context of practice-based Ph.D. research, perhaps its most important characteristics are: 1) an attentiveness to those ideas, and links between ideas, which guide or orient developments in the studio, and 2) an assessment of the relationship between the researcher's practice and the history (or histories) of the relevant ideas. For example, a Ph.D. examining painting's response to digital imagery is going to involve an examination of the kinds of imagery which might

Clive Cazeaux

belong to each category, as well as an appraisal of how these kinds are upset or fused due to the degree of borrowing and appropriation which takes place between them. These transformations might be contextualized historically in terms of the revolutions in image-making which took place from romanticism through expressionism to minimalism. Already, with these investigations, a terrific amount of aesthetic description and interpretation is called for in order to determine the kinds of image which might belong to each way of working.

The relevance of Sartre to art theory here, I aver, is due to the fact that his theory of language shows how description (in our case) of art can expand the cognitive possibilities which are seen in a work. The role of the concept, on this account, is not to contain its object but to create a ripple that brings a forgotten or unforeseen aspect of the work to light. As such, new or additional points of significance are created which can magnify or multiply the extent to which the work might be viewed from a theoretical perspective. This claim might seem to raise the issue of whether or not meaning is 'in' a work or read 'onto' it. Isn't Sartre's account (the objection might run) in danger of amounting to the claim that anything can said of a work? I don't think so, primarily because of the existential significance he attaches to writing. The object, for Sartre, is not something which opposes description or alienates the writer but something which establishes a moral contract between itself and consciousness. I say 'moral' because the metaphors that best describe the relationship come from the sphere of social interaction: objects 'invite', 'motivate', 'demand', or 'resist' description. Whether one is confronting a bottle of ink, a tree-root, or a painting, objects can only give themselves to the viewer incompletely and, therefore, in a way that requests or demands supplementation from her. The exchange is not necessarily a harmonious one, though. Finding the *right* word is often as difficult as deciding upon the *right* course of action. Similarly, Roquentin's moment of revelation at the end of *Nausea*, when his hand seems to become a crab and then a fish, is not beautiful but sublime. As Sartre has shown, there can be no moment of self-present, necessary correspondence between word and thing. One has to make a representation, choose a course of action.

Another way of making this point is to recognize that many of the aesthetic judgements we make about art are metaphorical or belong to a chain of thought in which we are reassessing the use of our categories. Metaphor and the reassessment of categories are closely linked in that the former is widely regarded as the cognitive principle whereby a category is borrowed from one domain in order to be ascribed to another to which it does not *literally* or *conventionally* apply. Familiar examples of metaphorical judgements about art are descriptions of paintings in terms of emotion, sculptures in terms of movement, and soundscapes in terms of texture or architecture (e.g. the sound embraced me). As regards reflection on our application of categories, I am thinking here of aesthetic encounters when the work unsettles or destabilizes our perception and we are required to construct new conceptual mappings in order to get a purchase on the work. This is often the case with the 'juxtapositional' genres of Dada, surrealism, the installation, and the ready-made. These metaphorical judgements reflect the moral question of finding the right word in as much as the production of metaphor is a fundamentally ethical act: it is a creative use of language on the part of the individual which nevertheless, in order for it to work and be recognized as a metaphor, has to be sensitive to the linguistic and cultural associations which the hearers or readers of the metaphor are likely to share.

One of the main problems of epistemology is that we are always 'at a remove' from things, that there is always a gap between the world and our knowledge of it. What Sartre does is show that this state of affairs is a condition of our rootedness in the world and not a deficiency which has to be overcome. When dealing with the situation in which we find ourselves, Sartre asserts, we cannot expect the conceptual to determine or capture completely the particularity of the event. The structure of experience is such that a nothingness always insinuates itself between past and present, between concept and action, between description and experience, keeping the two apart. This structure, as I have shown, is particularly evident in writing: the descriptive sentence creates a specificity which cannot possibly be identical with experience. The significance of this for the theory-practice debate is that it changes the way we think of studio practice and art theory as *kinds* of activity. Whereas traditional Platonic or Cartesian epistemologies prompt us to regard *making* and *talking about making* as two entirely separate activities, Sartre's existentialism presents them as parallel and related processes in so far as they both create gaps or saliences in an otherwise uniform flow of experience. These gaps, as far as the existentialist is concerned, represent the interruptions in the subject-object relationship (following Kant and Nietzsche) which disengage subjectivity from the brute causal order of the world, and which thereby allow the subject to orient themselves in the world.

Within this, perhaps the largest shift in perspective made by Sartre is with regard to our perception of the status of writing in art theory. Just how an artist/researcher decides to describe their work, to claim significance for a particular way of working, to select the associations they bring to their art, will influence the way in which the work contributes to theoretical debate. This, I have argued, is because a work of art is always a work under interpretation. Sartre is instructive here because he gives us a theory of description which shows how the choices we make in forming sentences actually determine which aspects (in our case) of a work stand out or sink below the surface. Putting a situation 'into words', for Sartre (note how the Aristotelian container model of the concept still informs our vocabulary), far from being a mere reductive gesture of containment, in actual fact alters the situation: it confers a level of specificity which is not present in the original moment, and thereby causes something either to stand up or drop away in the cognitive relationship between subject and object. On this account, description becomes almost like sculpture in that each sentence, each metaphor, each turn of phrase, chisels away at our perception of the work. As a result, determining the identity of the work, the aspect of the work which the artist selects as being most prominent for their theoretical enquiry, is seen to involve the same constructive, salience-creating decisions as the process of making itself.

While it is important to remember that theory and practice are distinct operations, what I have shown is that this distinction is not necessarily an oppositional or antithetical one. Rather, a theory *of theory* is possible which shows that the conceptual perspectives adopted in relation to art, together with all the decisions involved in arriving at these perspectives, can have a more vivid and tangible impact on the form and identity of a work than Aristotle's container logic would have us believe.

Clive Cazeaux

Painting: *Poignancy and Ethics*

Jim Mooney

Abstract

This brief paper sets out some speculative propositions which arise from the experience of the encounter with painting, both as producer and spectator. In particular, it seeks to expand upon the event of being 'moved' by painting and seeks to register the shift in inclination which is enacted through this movement. It investigates, albeit in a provisional form, the affect of poignancy and the way in which the poignant might be said to be stirred by loss and the way in which particular kinds of loss intersect with the more generic condition of loss which is a defining characteristic of painting. It proposes that the poignant acts as a catalyst which prepares the ground for the reception of previously unforeseen, and more proximal, intersubjective relations. The encounter with painting is proposed as a minor, but nevertheless significant, corollary to the 'Face to Face', the exorbitant demand which Emmanuel Levinas proposed as the very foundational event of ethics.

1 The condition of painting: How is painting doing?

Painting is a carcass right now - it has been picked clean of all its meat ...
painting has always been about death.
(Lari Pittman)[1]

This text seeks to explore questions which gather around the contemporary condition of painting and impact upon its future relevance as a vital and revitalized practice. The first of these questions, 'How is painting doing?' is deliberately posed in the convention we might use to enquire after an ailing friend or acquaintance. Thoughts on the state of painting's health inevitably arise in response to the seemingly perennial annunciation of its death or, at the very least, its terminal decline. It would indeed seem that when we begin to reflect upon painting thoughts of death, mortality, and finitude rarely lag far behind. Painting does indeed appear to enjoy a particularly entangled, intimate, and long-standing relation to death. However, this relation might not be as morbid or settled as it first appears; instead it is a relation in endless ferment, still highly relevant, fascinating, and capable of powerful illumination. It is this more profound relation to death which, paradoxically lends painting its continued life force and defiant resistance to the writers of its many obituaries. The kind of question which seeks a response in the second section of this paper would approximate something like, 'What is painting doing?', 'What can painting do?' or even 'What is left for painting to do?'; but most keenly, the steering question which emerges is: 'What is our relation to painting?', especially indeed if, as Pittman asserts, it has been picked clean of its meat!

Death, of course, is not an event that we can ever know. In any case, it would be folly to think of death as a singular event. The only deaths we *can* experience are

1   Lari Pittman, Gallery Talk at Rosamund Felsen Gallery, 4 December 1993.

2   Sigmund Freud,
    'Mourning and
    Melancholia', Penguin
    Freud Library, Vol. 11,
    On Metapsychology:
    The Theory of
    Psychoanalysis, London:
    Penguin Books, 1991,
    p. 253.

those deaths which unfold in life, which block living in life. We know our lives to be shaped by bereavements of all sorts, indeed, we metabolize bereavements slowly and they come to form part of who we are and who we will become. Culturally, however, it is the painter who has had to survive more than most. The painter has had to devise ways of facing the bereavement which follows on from the apparently interminable pronouncements of the death of the very practice which lends to her or him the name 'painter'. Some cultural commentators would have us believe that painting, if it is to have a continued cultural role, needs to open itself to various forms of contamination by other, purportedly more vital, practices in order to renew and extend its own vitality, in a somewhat forlorn bid to secure a foothold in the future. The demand is that painting move from some notional and moribund purity to a condition of fashionable hybridity, where painting is dilated and brings other modes of practice under the purview of its discourse. I have considerable sympathy for this ambition to reshape the territory of painting and there is no doubt something to be said for its advocacy, but I do question the ease with which this proposition is advanced as a sort of cure-all rescue remedy. I would propose that the more pressing and arguably, the more challenging exigency, would be to revitalize our *understanding* of painting. As we well know, painting has triumphantly survived these various death knells.

But how?

I'd like to propose that painting's survival is secured by a certain *failure* which is *the failure to mourn*. This failure to mourn arises from the painter's inability to detach his or her libido from the dead body of painting. Consequently, a pathological condition takes hold which prohibits the decathexis necessary to abandon this love object and wholly return to the world of the living. This condition is known to us as melancholia; a condition whereby we enter into an exhausting, yet never exhausted, dialogue with the dead. It is of course Freud who famously establishes a correlation between mourning and melancholia in his 1917 essay of the same name. In this essay he reveals to us a terrible yet necessary truth, that:

> '... it is a matter of general observation that people never
> willingly abandon a libidinal position, not even, indeed,
> when a substitute is already beckoning to them'.[2]

Freud

It wouldn't be a difficult undertaking to cite the array of contemporary art practices which beckon the painter, yet, obstinately, painters provide testimony to their possession by a body which is both the object and site of a failed or partial mourning. The temptation to be seduced by these other, supposedly, more vital practices, has proved to be too great for many, myself included, but not so for the painters who press ahead in their pursuits. They remain true to their first identificatory love and appear determined to kiss painting back to life. This wilful inability to let go, to relinquish possession, represents a significant victory for painting in the fraught and interminable struggle between the ego and the lost object. There is a considerable degree of ambivalence inherent in this relation and this ambivalence might be characterized as a kind of 'essential strife' in which the painter oscillates between hate and love, between a murderous desire to 'loosen the

Jim Mooney

fixation of the libido to the object'[3] and the contrary desire to nourish this affective fixation. This latter desire is expressed through the work of the theoretically engaged painter as an act of obsessive, *repeated reflection,* on the condition of the practice. This work of repeated reflection unfolds in the tenebrous space of liminality which the painter has come to inhabit with the love object. Contemporary painters, through their own specific concerns and motivations, knowingly or unknowingly, enter into an extended dialogue with the condemned body of painting, which inevitably invokes its long, distinguished *and* degraded history. Successful mourning would allow these painters to bring the dialogue to a close, to walk away, unburdened and untroubled, the body laid to rest. Instead, they are trapped by their failed work of mourning, which, in turn, initiates an interminable dialogue in which matters of praxis become endlessly complicated and, importantly, the most challenging of contemporary painters spur us on to revitalize the ways in which we 'think' and come to 'understand' the function of painting.

Admittedly, to speak of 'Painting' in the generic sense is a fraught business given the fractal intricacies which have come to characterize the contemporary operations of painters. Yet, there are nevertheless general remarks which can be made with regard to the function of painting to which a degree of cultural worth still attaches. It is perhaps a commonplace to assert that painting, in common with other aesthetic productions, simultaneously marks and is marked by loss. Nevertheless, it is such a fundamental condition that it is worth reiterating that the loss of the 'originary' love object provides the painter with a necessary and vital generative impetus. Moreover, the kind of painting which furnishes us with images, functions, in part, *commemoratively,* and although not strictly speaking indexical, nevertheless points an index finger, as it were, to the object which the painted image now comes to substitute and resemble.

Crucially, painting is both of this world and yet simultaneously *posits* a world 'in itself', that is, a world decisively separated but nevertheless extricated from this world. In this sense it enacts a double occupancy, being both an object in this world and presenting to us a world 'in itself' where things are extracted from this world and are accorded an *exotic* positioning; exotic, in the etymological sense of 'outside', *dehors,* apart from. This notion of a double occupancy brings to mind Maurice Blanchot's radical likening of the status of the image to that of the cadaver which, we are instructed, is uncannily both here and nowhere. It is Blanchot who teaches us that this privileged non-site is shared by both the cadaverous presence, (the presence of the unknown), and the image. He writes:

'The image does not, at first glance, resemble the corpse
but the cadaver's strangeness is perhaps also that of the
image.'[4]

Blanchot

The appearance of the image, in common with that of the cadaver, depends on an immensely fragile and disturbing *doubling* and, most poignantly, is what is left behind when the object it resembles is gone. The work of the painter engages in the delicate process of creating apparitions which can occasionally glow and cast illumination upon this otherwise abandoned ground of dereliction.

In a particular sense, the image assumes a mediating role between the subject (viewer) and the object to which it refers. Viewed in this way, the painted substrate,

3 *ibid.*, p. 267.

4 Maurice Blanchot, 'The Two Versions of the Imaginary', *The Space of Literature*, Lincoln and London: University of Nebraska Press, 1982, p. 256.

5   Jacques Lacan, 'What is a Picture?', *The Four Fundamental Concepts of Psycho-Analysis*, trans. Alan Sheridan, London: Penguin Books, 1977, p. 108.

6   Alphonso Lingis, 'Imperative Surfaces', *Foreign Bodies*, New York and London: Routledge, 1994.

7   Michael Inwood, *Heidegger*, Oxford and New York: Oxford University Press, 1997, p. 48.

8   Alphonso Lingis, *Foreign Bodies*, New York and London: Routledge, 1994, p. 217.

the *surface*, facilitates and proposes this mediation. I prefer, however, to consider the carefully factured surface in terms of a differentially inclined spatial and temporal movement from inwardness to exteriority. Indeed, this very movement is the experience which I most value when I stand before a painting and the experience I most seek without ever knowing precisely what it is I seek. It is the movement which guarantees the renewal and continued cultural currency of painting. My face turns to an exteriority, to the surface of things beyond in the transcendent spaces of the world.

I'd like to mention here Lacan's proposition cited in the 'Four Fundamental Concepts' that ' ... in front of the picture, I am elided as subject of the geometrical plane'[5] and, if there is any merit to be found in this statement, we might fairly extend the proposition to include the painter of the picture, asserting that the screen (the geometrical plane of the canvas) now be seen as the locus of mediation between subjects, becoming a tenuous, fragile and luminous site of intersubjective exchange. We are dealing here with surfaces which face us with radically different tensions and functions which often operate simultaneously. We respond to what Alphonso Lingis calls *imperative surfaces*.[6] A surface might be wilfully hard, smooth and unyielding, equally it may be softly toothsome and absorbent, it might present a barrier to be overcome or negotiated or alternatively, it could offer an entirely welcoming and permeable skin. It could equally well be all that there is: pure surface. The surface might be virginal as in a *tabula rasa* or again, it may carry the heavy burden of saturated inscription. It can stand as the only glimpse we can apprehend of what lies behind or it can act as an aperture or passageway through to what has previously been entirely occluded. I am prompted to consider the painted surface as akin to the face of another and can be perceived as the exposed surface of a depth structure. The surface may well be all of these things, tessellated into a tightly woven mosaic of varying tensions and densities. However, let us remind ourselves that, in every case the surface, the (sur)face, is that which is most exposed and let us consider, in this light, Heidegger's formulation of truth as ' ... uncovering and uncoveredness, shedding light and light shed'.[7] This shedding of light on the uncovered, the exposure of the exposed face, produces a vulnerability which appeals, (the call of the vulnerable), bringing nakedness to the surface. Standing before a painting, when conditions permit, we respond to the naked appeal of this surface and are beckoned, called upon to enter into a relation which is not nearly as forbidding, but is, nevertheless, akin to that which Levinas calls the 'face-to-face'. According to Levinas, the face is the invisible that summons from the distance of alterity. Lingis describes it as follows:

> The face and surfaces of others afflict me, cleave to me, sear me. They
> solicit me, press their needs on me; they direct me, order me. The
> face of a stranger in the crowd turned to me is an imposition. The face
> of a Somalian looking at me from a newspaper intrudes into my zone
> of implantation; I am relieved that the opaqueness of the paper screens
> me from him. In the corridors of my projects, my goals, and my reasons,
> the tormented laughter of the visionary and of the one lost in orgasmic
> abysses arrests my advance.[8]

Lingis

Jim Mooney

The face-to-face relation carries the promise and demand of the possibility of radically reducing the distance which separates the Same from the Other. A proximity born in response to a beckoning distance, establishes itself, and takes up a precariously identified, quivering, position. Levinas writes:

'The Other becomes my neighbour precisely through the way the face summons me, calls for me, begs for me, and in so doing recalls my responsibility, and calls me into question.'[9]

Levinas

This call to respond solicits a movement which is both an inclination (a leaning toward) and a shift in inclination, that is, a shift in taste, a shift in disposition.

2 Poignancy and ethics: What is our relation to painting?

Following on from the preceding section which posed the question 'How is painting doing?', this section could well be subtitled will 'What is our relation to painting?' I will open with a germinal quotation from Roland Barthes:

'A photograph's punctum is that accident which pricks me (but also bruises me, is poignant to me)'.[10]

Barthes

Poignancy *moves* us and the movement it gives rise to, leans us toward the Other and inclines us toward the condition of 'implication' where the Same and the Other become entwined, enfolded, enlaced. It is the *sting* of poignancy which enables such a shift; we lurch, move outside ourselves, and are briefly enveloped in the rapture of the ecstatic. This can never be expected or guaranteed, it may be sought out or hoped for, but almost always happens by accident and mostly when we are least prepared. When it does occur, it is experienced as an irrecoverable instant, a moment when our subjectivity is stretched beyond the confines of the familiar, and reaches out, gravitating toward the object of its longing. It is perhaps worth underscoring here the trace of the Greek *ektasis* ('stretching'), through *ekstasis* ('to make to stand'), which remains resonant in the *ecstatic*. Moreover, and more importantly, according to Levinas it is:

'Through ecstasy (that) man takes up existence. Ecstasy is then found to be the very event of existence'.[11]

Levinas

Language can inhabit thought in ways which blind us to its treacherous deceit, concealing its other face in our usual patterns and habits of speech and I suspect we have become all too habituated to using the term 'poignancy' in sentimental response to the pathetic scene and tend to overlook the subtle violence of which it also speaks. I would ask that we remember the semantic determinants of 'poignancy', which pertain to weapons, and signify something as being painfully sharp and piercing. With this in mind, if, for example, we take a foil, the type of sword used in competition which inflicts a *sting* as opposed to a mortal wound, and consider the disturbance it provokes, we inch ever closer to the establishment of an approximation between poignancy and Roland Barthes' articulation of the

9   Emmanuel Levinas, 'Ethics as First Philosophy', *The Levinas Reader*, ed. Sean Hand, Oxford: Blackwell, 1989, p. 83.

10 Roland Barthes, *Camera Lucida: Reflections on Photography*, London: Fontana Paperbacks,1984, p. 27.

11 Emmanuel Levinas, *Existence and Existents*, trans. Alphonso Lingis, Dordrecht, Boston and London: Kluwer Academic Publishers, 3rd printing, 1995, pp. 81-82.

12 *ibid.*, p. 95.

13 *ibid.*, p. 95.

'punctum'. Most daringly, we might propose that we arrive at the insinuating intricacies of an ethics of the punctum. The punctum as ethical event? Might we audaciously nudge this idea along and formulate the proposition that it is *poignancy* which introduces the punctum, (by now almost worn-out, tired and degraded, through discussions in relation to the photograph), to painting, where it becomes lodged in the very depths of its surface?

It is due to a mobilizing sympathy, aroused by poignancy, that the work becomes folded back, returned to us, incorporated once more into our world. An ethical event of this kind produces an 'initial asymmetrical intersubjectivity',[12] when recognition of the Other's subjectivity is unevenly tilted, that is, until the moment poignancy produces its *sting,* in an instant, and a sympathetic movement is initiated which inclines us in another direction: toward 'the leaving of an inwardness for an exteriority'.[13] This event, in the order of events, is perhaps small, almost imperceptible, surreptitious even, and threatens to fade into the obscure if it were not also talked of as the very founding event of existence.

This inclination, this departure from 'an inwardness to an exteriority', can be said to typify the operations of the painter as much as it could be said to describe the viewer's relation as respondent to the appellant, to the work of the painter. Consequently, we may ask if it be licit to consider that viewer and painter do no more than collude in order to create the conditions under which the work does the work's work? This double investment, this two-sided operation, speaks of a libidinous economy whereby the planar surface of the work becomes no more and no less than the site of a concentrated intersubjective exchange. This privileged site initiates a flow of grace and we might well deduce that the particular gift of the work is a gift which conveys the grace of poignancy and the poignancy of grace. I have in mind here, the shed, shared, light of grace which flows from the ecstatic.

The work solicits our sympathy, our attention, and should we fall under the sway of its mute epiphany, and hear the muffled call to respond, a blossoming occurs, whereby an improbable organ of affectivity unfurls, which by some small miracle, reflects, as in a mirror, the very organ of affectivity which gave rise to the work in the first instance. In this way, the semblance of an intersubjective symmetry makes its appearance. Perhaps to speak of an organ of affectivity misleads, or leastways leads us in another direction, and I am persuaded to introduce a certain rigour which would dislodge this fancy and guide us to alight upon the notion of another improbable organ: the organ of the libido.

All painting demands to be apprehended in terms of its own seductive allure, its own particular capacity to present itself to us as 'a significant thing', and this is entirely appropriate. We are therefore pressed to attend to the specifics of the painted surface, the particular way in which matter is pleated and most especially, to the interlacing of matter and libido.

Lacan designates a name for this organ which is not an organ in the normal sense, inasmuch as it does not require the usual nourishments and, by dint of this fact, is considered immortal. He calls it the 'lamella'. The lamella is characterized by an extreme flatness. It moves around a lot, flying in every direction. It has the capacity to adhere and to insinuate. It can overwhelm. It can smother. It can, of course, adhere to the surface of a painting, and then again, it can fly off. It might even strike us in the face! It sticks to painting in the way painters stick to painting. It is the very glue, the sticky substance of *jouissance* which fixes the painter on painting. It is clear we don't have much choice in the matter. We are bonded, by

Jim Mooney

something *like* the bonds of love, to a practice which refuses to relinquish its hold. The painter is held in thrall by this interminable libidinal fixation. We, as viewers, as respondents, are in turn, enthralled by these libidinally charged surfaces which solicit and soak up some of our own libidinal pulsions. Poignancy, then, gives rise to the ethical and the libidinal in a bid to stir, to implicate our capacity to care; to respond to the call of the Other. We become implicated through an overcoming of the indifference which stifles response. This implication in the alterity of the Other, moves us toward a questioning of our own subject positions and instigates a shift in our own capacity for recognition and it might be helpful here to recount that according to Levinas:

14 Cited by Alphonso Lingis, *Foreign Bodies,* New York and London: Routledge, 1994, p. 223.

> ' ... alterity is the region where the other, susceptible and vulnerable,
> abides in mortality'.[14]

Levinas

The dynamic oscillation between proximity and distance, provoked by this encounter, introduces subtle erotic modalities which place us, as subjects, under pressure. This pressure arises from the disturbance carried in the train of the demand to effect a repositioning, enact a shift in inclination, as we ready ourselves to face the work's face.

This work of 'facing' is more challenging than we might at first imagine. The first challenge is to 'sovereignty', to the very notion of a *sovereign* subject. And if this challenge is effective, it opens us to a stateless 'state of being', to a place where we are suddenly assailable, responsive, vulnerable, and questioning. The comfort of an illusory stasis of Being cedes to the more troubling flux of new becomings. When most effective *and* affective, paintings represent the presences of absences which have the power to marshal all of our other absences and bring them, sometimes cruelly, before our very presence. We are in this way, *called to account;* called to account for our presence in the fullness of this alterity, this presence/absence of the Other.

Concrete abstractions – a Della Volpean perspective on studio practice as research

Kenneth G. Hay

Abstract

The Ph.D. in Studio Practice at the University of Leeds was set up on broadly Della Volpean lines. The programme is intended to embody and enable the dialectical interrelation of practical theory and theoretical practice so as to recognize the concrete materiality of studio practice as research, rather than envisaging studio work existing with an (often) under-theorized theory of theory 'bolted on' as cognitive support or intellectual crutch. The aim was to create an experimental space for high-level studio research, where the research-as-artwork would be recognized as cognitively equivalent, if methodologically and generically distinct, from research in other doctoral areas where the textual is the norm. This is not of course to preclude that a studio practice might indeed be primarily 'textual', but merely to emphasize the dialectics at play. In this conception, the work of the Italian philosopher Galvano Della Volpe (1895-1968) has served as a very useful methodological mentor. Della Volpe's work, mostly untranslated into English, encompassed three interrelating fields: moral philosophy, philosophical logic, and materialist aesthetics. The author takes the interrelations amongst these apparently discrete areas as paradigmatic of a method of conceiving studio work as material practice, on a par with, if distinct from, other epistemological areas such as the sciences.

1 The poet C.S. Calverley's response to his Dean to explain the ruckus resulting from Calverley being chased to his lodgings in Oxford by an irate pub owner after having stolen his pub sign. From a BBC Radio 3 Broadcast on C.S.Calverley, 1973.

Sir, an evil and adulterous generation seeketh after a sign, and there shall no sign be given it.[1]

The University of Leeds Ph.D. in Studio Practice, established with generous funding from the Burton family in 1995, was developed and inspired – at least in my mind – around the work of Della Volpe. Della Volpe's reworking of the materialist logic behind Marx's 'Kapital', in particular, the C-A-C' circle, which starts with the analysis of the concrete, material world (C) from which analysis abstractions are formed through which to theorize the world (A); which abstractions, being concrete, in turn go back into and 'interfere' with the concrete world once more (C'), setting off a new process of conceptualization. This circle articulates an intellectual journey which metaphorizes the hermeneutic movement from (for example) haystack, to Monet's stare, to the touch of yellow pigment on the canvas, and then from canvas to spectator/critic to conceptual understanding, to complete the hermeneutic chain. It can be poetically grasped in Eliot's image of the rose transfigured by auto consciousness ('the rose has the look of a rose that is looked at'), or materially exemplified in Lenin's materialist explanation of how something as apparently 'transparent' as a glass of water inevitably includes the history of how the glass was made, who turned on the tap, who laid the pipes, who dug the trenches - i.e. it is an inevitably and irretrievably *social* history, without which the glass of water becomes (historically) 'opaque' (the opacity of non-historicized 'seeing' - or idealist 'non-

JVAP 2 (1&2) 64–77 ©Intellect Ltd 2002

seeing'). The sense of circularity is illusory. The movement of thought from the concrete to abstract and back into the concrete is not an identical return, but altered and enriched by the journey. An apple once seen by Cézanne, Courbet or Giacommetti is not the same apple as we saw before, but carries the 'look of an apple that is looked at' and our world is changed forever.

This then is the challenge posed by the Ph.D. in Studio Practice, and let us meet it head on: How to forge a materialist (art) practice/set of practices through which the opacity of non-historical seeing (idealist non-seeing) can be rendered limpid and transparent? And once forged, how to go on pushing back the creeping reification which threatens to set in, like rigor mortis, to the new found dialectical freedom of an intellectual body in motion, unfettered by past misconceptions and ideological blind spots. And how to keep this body in motion.

The Ph.D. emerged from an on-going dialogue with my colleague at Leeds, Terry Atkinson, and was materially developed by my former colleague Susan Taylor. We all shared a commitment to the concrete materiality of art practice as discourse, and a firm if critical commitment to the excellence of the firm integration of theoretical practice and practical theory as inescapable and indeed, fully desirable components of a materialist set of practices in studio work and art theory/history which T.J. Clark inaugurated there in 1975. Terry was coming from his background in and subsequent move away from Art & Language, his work on cognition and various experiments with 'disaffirmative practices'. I was coming from my own research into German idealist and materialist aesthetics, and subsequent long involvement in Italian materialism, from Spaventa, Labriola and De Sanctis, through to Croce, Gramsci and Della Volpe - the philosophical tradition of the Neapolitan Hegelian School and its subsequent materialist reincarnation in the cultural politics of the PCI (Italian Communist Party) in the 1960s and 1970s. Susan Taylor's practices explored the, often physical and always material, interfaces of photographic imagery, sound installation, embodiment and spatialization.

The Ph.D. was forged out of a sense that we wanted to create a 'front-line' space for advanced artistic practice(s) which would recognize its concrete intellectuality, its cognitive import, its complexity, its right to be taken seriously as thought, its epistemological equality in comparison to other branches of the humanities, in short its value as research. The programme is very small - initially we took one or two students per annum. With the recent merger with Bretton Hall (2001), numbers have increased to around five or six. It is thus very focused. Throughout, we have held onto a very particular vision of what we think a studio Ph.D. is, and we have had to fight quite hard, even within our own institution to maintain our vision of the specific integration of theorized practice, and in particular the fluid relation operating between the practical and written component which is characteristic of the Leeds programme.

In addition to the on-going debate between Terry and myself as to the relationship between the visual and the verbal, one of the notions behind the Ph.D. in Studio Practice at Leeds, was the question: How does Academe cope with the existence of artists within its structures? Mischieviously and anachronistically put: How would Vermeer, Rembrandt, or Cézanne have fared if they'd had to be included in the RAE submissions? Not noted for their publications; didn't travel much or give papers to conferences; didn't feature in the citations index until some time after their deaths; weren't particularly loquacious; didn't have many shows outside their home town. So are we saying that they didn't contribute to culture, or that their lives' work cannot be understood as 'research', that it had no suitable outcomes, no appropriate methodology, no contribution to human understanding of, as Jonathan Miller has said, 'what it is to *be* in the world'? Or is not the response to these non-questions rather, as Wittgenstein would respond, that we are asking the wrong questions: 'Why is it that dogs tell no lies? Is it that they are too honest?' Undoubtedly funding bodies such as the HEFCE have moved some way in beginning to formulate some ways in which some categories of art-making might fit some rubric of fundability. But such attempts seem inevitably to be hoist on their own intellectually barren petard. If more and more artistic practices are seemingly able to be matched to more or more adequate categories of fundability, this is not to say that the world is being enriched by better and better artworks, merely that more and more art-makers are learning to match/distort their practices to the categories expected for fundability. (The Soviet Writer's Guild operated a similar system in the 1930s). A rise in RAE 'scores' does not necessarily signify an increase in research 'quality' or even activity, (since not all 'activity' is recognized as research) but simply that institutions and intellectuals-in-waiting are getting better at matching themselves to the rubrics of operational expectability so as to receive financial rewards. This is Pavlovian rather than enlightened.

There are two possible responses to this provocation: Conservatively, and idealistically, like Plato, one can argue that artists do not belong in the intellectual Republic of Academe. What they do is not research and cannot be measured or appraised as such. They should go back to the old art schools and conservatoires and return to mumbling about ineffable beauty, transcendent truth and significant form. Alternatively, one (enlightened, materialist), can argue that Academe needs to rethink its categorical distinctions so as to encompass and embrace the intellectual otherness of art practice. For art practitioners, there is a real sense in which art practice is 'front line' research, constitutive of new knowledge about the world, where art history/theory is secondary, reflective knowledge, produced post-artistic-factum. How is it that the latter can be comfortably appraised as research but not the former? What signs of research activity are missing?

Let us put our money where our mouth is and declare unambiguously that art work *is* intellectual; that artists require as much specialist training, background reading, lateral thinking, experience, learning skills, applied methodologies, and can carry as much cognitive weight and often as many years of formal education, as nuclear scientists, experimental psychologists, mechanical engineers, etc. This is not to say that everyone who attempts to make art is an artist, anymore than to declare every student of physics an Einstein. Seen as what Gramsci would term a praxis, art working is on a par with, but generically different from, other intellectual domains such as History (including its sub-set Art History), Philosophy and Letters. With Della Volpe, as outlined below, I am also sympathetic to the view that art practice can be aligned with scientific research, as mutually coexistent equals, again with the proviso that each domain is cognitively, semantically and methodologically distinct, and contributes to knowledge in different, generically specific ways.

Within the confines of this paper, I will merely touch upon three aspects of Della Volpe's work which help to inform the complexities and specificities of recognizing art practice as theory, and which, in turn inform the ambition of the Leeds Studio Practice Ph.D. namely: translatability, 'concrete' or 'determinate abstraction' and (filmic) metaphor.

Kenneth G. Hay

Translatability

> In all language and linguistic creations there remains in addition to what can be conveyed, something that cannot be communicated. (W. Benjamin)[2]

From Horace's day onwards there have been many attempts to categorize the various forms of art into distinct 'genres' and to individuate their specific competencies.[3] One of the most straightforward methods of conceptualizing the specificity of these genres is to attempt a translation from one genre to another and, as Benjamin points out, to thereby observe what gets lost 'in transit'. The danger in so doing is to reassert the old idealist chestnut of the 'ineffability' of art - that there exists, in some abstract realm, what Goethe called an *urphänomen*, a potential phenomenon waiting to be given form. Such a notion sponsors an Ideal, ultimately inexplicable art, which 'passeth our understanding'. Such is not my project here. It is one of Benjamin's many paradoxes that while asserting a materialist aesthetic of production he yet believed in the existence of a Cabalistic version of Goethe's *urphänomen*, but that is another story.[4]

Roman Jakobson argues for a distinction to be drawn between three types of translation.[5] There is, firstly what he terms 'intralingual translation' or simple paraphrase, where we interpret one verbal sign by means of other verbal signs of the same language. For example when we give an explanation of an unknown word. Secondly there is what he calls, 'interlingual translation' or translation in the normal sense and the practice in which Benjamin himself was involved - the interpretation of a verbal sign with the aid of another language. But thirdly, and most relevant for my discussion today is what Jakobson called 'intersemiotic translation': the interpretation of a linguistic sign with the help of a non-verbal sign system (or vice versa: the interpretation of a non-verbal sign with the help of a verbal sign, such as the verbal description of a ballet or a painting).

In addition to these cultural and linguistic differences common to most translations, the task of the translator who would attempt a translation between genres also has to take on board the more complex incongruities of different semiotic structures each with its own histories and traditions.[6] It is particularly this type of 'translation' and these sorts of difficulties which preoccupied the Italian philosopher Galvano Della Volpe (1895-1968) throughout his aesthetic reflection, which particularly illuminate the distinctiveness of art practices as constitutive of knowledge and research.

Words and images - an uneasy dialectic[7]

> Why should a description, which is admirable in a poem become ridiculous in a painting? ... Why should the god (Neptune) whose head is so majestic in the poem (Aeneid 1: 126-27) - rising out of the waves, look like a decapitated head in a painting of the scene? How is it that something which is pleasing to our minds is yet displeasing to our eyes?[8]

> Why can't a dog simulate pain? Is he too *honest*?[9]

2 W. Benjamin, 'The Task of the Translator', in *Illuminations*, trans. Harry Zohn, London: Fontana, 1976, pp. 69-82, p. 79.

3 cf. R.W Lee, 'Ut Pictura Poesis: The Humanistic Theory of Painting', in *Art Bulletin*, pp. 196-269.

4 cf. 'Introduction', by K.G. Hay to Walter Benjamin and Wolff Zucker, 'Pay rise? You must be Joking!', a short Radio play, first English trans. S. Alagapan, *The Tempest*, vol. 1, no 1, Leeds, 1993.

5 Roman Jakobson, 'Linguistiche Aspekte der Übersetzung', in *Übersetzungswissenschaft*, ed. Wolfram Wilss, Darmstadt, 1981, pp. 189-98.

6 Tadashi Ogawa, in a recent article on translation argues that: 'Any translation presupposes two sorts of invariance, which we might refer to as inter-cultural and interlingual respectively - these two sorts of invariance have to be brought to light in the process of translation', in Tadashi Ogawa, 'Translation as a cultural-philosophic problem: Towards a phenomenology of culture', in *The Monist*, vol. 78, no. 1, pp. 18-29.

7 Some themes touched upon here appeared in K.G. Hay, 'Generic Specificity and the Problem of Translation in Della Volpe', in *Text and Visuality*, Word & Image Interactions, III,

ed. Martin Heuser, Amsterdam and Atlanta, 1999; and 'The Visual and the Verbal in Postmodern Practice: The Truisms of Jenny Holzer', in *Cynos : Image et Langage, Problèmes, Approches, Méthodes'*, vol. 11, no. 1, Centre de Recherche sur les Écritures de Langue Anglaise, Université de Nice, (1994), and formed part of a stimulating discussion day at the Courtauld Institute of Art, London, on 'Visual Narrative', on 22 March 1996.

8   Diderot, 'Lettre sur les sourds et muets', *Œuvres complètes de Denis Diderot*, vol. 4, Paris: Herman, 1978.

9   L. Wittgenstein, *Philosophical Remarks*, Oxford, 1940, § 250, p. 90e.

10 R.W Lee, 'Ut Pictura Poesis, The Humanistic Theory of Painting', *Art Bulletin*, pp. 196-269.

11 G.L. Lessing, *Laoköon, oder über die Grenzen der Malerei und Poesie*, 1766. I have developed these themes in 'Picturing Reading: Della Volpe and Lessing', special edition of *Paragraph* on Visual Narrative, UCL/University of Edinburgh Press, 1996 and in Helsinki, *Della Volpe, Lessing and Visual Narrative*, seminar for the Critical Theory Forum, Helsinki Academy of Art, Jan. 1997.

12 Lessing, *op. cit.*

13 Diderot, *op. cit.*

The tradition of unease or open conflict between the visual and the verbal stretches back a long way. Horace's famous simile, in the *Ars poetica*: 'Ut pictura poesis' (As in painting, so in poetry) in fact prioritized painting over verbal discourse, by holding up the former as the example on which the latter is modelled. As R.W Lee has argued, the dictum has been consistently mistranslated by theorists on art from Horace's day onwards such that its reverse, 'As in poetry, so in painting', became the classic definition of the relationship between the arts, the legacy of which continues to cause confusion on the part of both theorists and practitioners alike.[10] This wilful historical mischief in fact reverses the priorities which Horace had clearly outlined, and makes of visual art a mere copy of words. I am not attempting here to 'redress the balance' (although the temptation as a practitioner is strong). To do so would be at best a reiteration of idealism, and at worst perverse, given the context of this paper. For, as is obvious, the debates concerning the classification of the various arts which followed from Horace's day have been further complicated by the fact that the medium in which they have been carried out through the centuries, and are still being carried out, has been, necessarily, that of verbal language, which itself constitutes the domain of several types of art: poetry, drama, the novel or prose poems, to name a few. It is this peculiar position of the verbal as 'master discourse' able to both constitute art, as well as the critical and analytic discourses about art, which has rendered the relationship between ordinary and poetic words, between words and music, words and dance, or, for the purposes of this talk, words and images, so complex, and for most practitioners and critics alike, so confusing.

The great idealist attempt to classify the arts and their various competencies was Gottfried Leopold Lessing's *Laoköon*, published in 1766.[11] For Lessing, Ariosto's poetry, for example, is overabundant in descriptive detail with the result that the purity of the poetic genre becomes clouded or clogged (*Laoköon*, XX). The central drive of the *Laoköon* was directed against just this type of artistic transgression, whether of poetry or of the figurative arts, that Horace's dictum 'Ut pictura poesis' might seem to encourage.

> When the Laocöon of Virgil shouts, who would consider that in order to shout he must have his mouth open and that this would render the figure ugly? It is enough that the 'clamores horrendos ad sidera tollit' appeals as a noble image to our ears and minds, and the visual aspect can be left to your imagination.[12]

In answer to Diderot's question; 'How is it that something which is pleasing to our minds, is yet displeasing to our eyes?'[13], Lessing replies with his system of categorical distinctions between the proper competencies of each genre. Painting can only do what painting can do; words follow different rules. It is as wrong to expect words to provide a precise equivalent for visual art as it is to expect poetry to be replaceable by dance, or architecture.

In the twentieth century, Benedetto Croce's *Aesthetic* (1905) was the last major attempt of Idealism to codify what he saw as the proper competencies of the abstractly separate realms of Art, Ethics and Logic.[14] For Croce, as indeed for formalist criticism from Clive Bell and Roger Fry through to the later Clement Greenberg, the visual was a distinct terrain from the verbal, which had to be grasped, ultimately, by intuition alone. 'Check in your mind with your umbrella, and go in with a naked, innocent eye', was Greenberg's comment on the recent Monet show at the Royal Academy in London.[15] Similarly, for Croce, the central feature of

Kenneth G. Hay

'art' is that it is not reducible to rational thought (logic), but takes the form of 'images' which have to be intuited 'internally' (in ways which are forever mysterious) by the receiver/viewer. The problematic nature of this apprehension (i.e. its claim to scientificity, its position as 'value-free' or 'non-ideological') is quickly glossed over by Croce in a thoroughly unsatisfactory way, by appealing to just that postulated 'common sense' which Gramsci was later to demythologize.[16] It is easy to see this as a return of the alienated bourgeois subject (or isolated existential monad) which materialism had effectively banished in the 1840s. As with Hegelian Idealism, Croce's romantic idealism stressed the primacy of (timeless) Mind or Spirit over what he saw as the 'brute' materiality of the real (socio-historical) world.[17]

Taking his inspiration from Aristotle's observation (in the *Poetics*) of the capacity of poetry to convey a rational historical content, the Italian philosopher Galvano Della Volpe produced a radical critique of both romanticism and idealism (whether of Hegelian or Crocean origins), and a critique of 'vulgar' materialist approaches which underestimated the formal-semantic autonomy of art, relying either on a crude socio-economic determinism or a form of 'contentism' (such as Lukàcs' theory of realism).[18] I have outlined elsewhere some of those aspects of Della Volpe's rich and unjustly neglected aesthetic theory relating to the problem of generic specificity and the problem of translation, with specific reference to his anti-Croceanism and his work on film.[19] Here I should just like to touch on his concept of 'determinate' or 'concrete abstraction' in relation to filmic metaphor as an example of the materialist analysis of non-verbal signifying practices can shed light on the problematic of how art contributes to knowledge, how this can be apprehended, and thereby offer some insight into and some suggestions as to what a materialist art-practice-as-research might entail.

Concrete or determinate abstractions - the plasticity of images

In August 1954, Della Volpe published a collection of ten essays on aesthetics in the 'Piccola biblioteca dello spettacolo' series, published by *Filmcritica*. To these were added a further five studies in the second edition, published as a special section of *Filmcritica* in the summer of 1962.[20] The book carried the two epigraphs from Diderot and Lessing, quoted above, relating to the classification of the arts by 'genres' and the difficulties in 'translating' one genre into another.[21] The essays, on film, ideology and the interrelation of the arts, centre around the 'problems of a scientific aesthetics', which involve the critique of Crocean idealism and all forms of 'a priorism', as well as of the shortcomings of post-Crocean materialist aesthetics, whether in Gramsci or Lukàcs, the specificity of filmic language in Pudovkin, Chaplin or Ciné-vérité and the relationship between ideology and art. Declaring the need for the 'rigorous development of an anti-romantic, anti-idealist' aesthetic, or 'an aesthetic of the means of expression', to counter critics like Moravia for whom the film was a 'crude' instrument compared to the pen, Della Volpe proposes a 'new Laocöon' which would recognize the diversity of artistic means of expression in a non-hierarchical way: their 'peaceful coexistence' as means of expression.[22] Horace's distinction between visual and verbal, seemed ever more gratuitous in the light of specifically 'filmic' (i.e. 'untranslatable') elements in Eisenstein, Groucho Marx or Chaplin. Della Volpe reiterates his repugnance for Croce's intuitive idealism, and proposes instead a theory, which recognizes the 'full intellectuality' of art, and acknowledges its 'full cognitive value.'[23] His is thus an anti-Kantian theory

14 B. Croce, *Aesthetic as General Linguistic and Science of Expression*, trans. D. Ainsley, London, 1905.

15 C. Greenberg, interviewed on *The Late Show*, BBC TV, 1991.

16 cf. Antonio Gramsci, *Selections from the Prison Notebooks*, ed. Quintin Hoare and David Forgacs, London, 1976.

17 For a more detailed discussion of this in relation to Italian Materialism from the Neapolitan Hegelians to Della Volpe, cf. K.G. Hay, 'Italian Materialist Aesthetics', unpublished Ph.D. thesis, University of Wales, 1990, and K.G. Hay, 'Bertrando Spaventa and Italian Hegelianism', paper for the Graduate Research Seminar, Department of Cultural Studies, University of Derby, 1995. On Della Volpe's Aesthetics, see K.G. Hay, 'Della Volpe's Critique of Romantic Aesthetics', in *Parallax*, vol. 1, no. 2, Leeds, 1996. For a discussion of Della Volpe's materialist logic see Ludovico Geymonat, 'La positività del molteplice', *Rivista di filosofia*, xlii, vi, no. 3, July-September 1951.

18 Aristotle, *Poetics*, 1451b, 1ff.

19 cf. K.G. Hay, 'Generic Specificity and the Problem of Translation in Della Volpe', *Word and Image Interactions III*, ed. Martin Heuser, Amsterdam and

Atlanta: Rodopi, 1999.

20 G. Della Volpe, 'Il verosimile filmico ed altri scritti di estetica', in *Filmcritica*, no. 121, p. 91, now in *Opere*, vol. 5, Rome: Editori Riuniti, 1972-73.

21 Diderot, 'Lettre sur les sourds et les muets'. Lessing, *Laoköon oder ueber die Grenzen der Malerie und Poesie*, 1766.

22 G. Della Volpe, *Opere*, vol. 6, *op. cit.*, p. 12; The expressions derive from Rudolph Arnheim and Umberto Barbaro respectively.

23 *ibid.*, p. 13.

24 *ibid.*, pp. 13-14.

25 i.e. Humboldt's dictum that the critic's task is to 'wander in the realms of the ineffable'.

26 St Augustine, *De gen ad. litt,*. IX, 47.

27 cf. K. Marx, 'Introduction', *Grundrisse*, trans. and ed. M. Nicolaus, Harmondsworth, 1973. I have discussed this elsewhere in relation to Antonio Labriola, K.G. Hay, 'Italian Materialist Aesthetics', 1990, *op. cit.*

which rejects the principle of the beautiful as an 'aesthetic idea' and which reasserts the positivity (and primacy) of the material world. Roughly summarized it proposes.

> that the representations given in a judgment, being empirical, are therefore also aesthetic, and that consequently any judgment which results from these representations is as logical as it is aesthetic, hence these representations are always referable back to the object.[24]

The aesthetic is *as* cognitive as science, because it is always rooted in, and gives knowledge of, the material world.

In *Estetica in nuce*, (Aesthetics in a nutshell) Croce had argued that the task of the critic or reader is to:

> ... unravel the individual history of the art-work and treat it, *not in relation to social [or civil] history, but as a world in itself* into which all of history flows from time to time, *transcended by power of the imagination* (my italics).

Della Volpe quizzes how this is possible if the intellectual and the aesthetic are two different realms, separated, as Croce says, by an 'abyss'. By underrating the concrete rationality of art, Croce reaffirms the Romantic-mystical view whereby art is seen as 'ineffable' (and thus not tenable as research).[25] Croce's affirmation of art as 'cosmic intuition' (or 'pure' ahistorical intuition) is really a dogmatic restatement of the neo-Platonic 'pure unity' whose apprehension would depend on a 'pure non-reflection' (i.e. 'thoughtlessness') or the 'aesthetic rapture' of neo-Platonic religious ecstasy. St Augustine had already shown that this type of experience, inasmuch as it pertained to the 'contingent' could not therefore be 'eternal' (or ahistorical).[26] However, an 'ineffable' art is one, to paraphrase Wittgenstein: 'about which one cannot speak', because devoid of concrete, historical content; if it is 'beyond history' then it must also be 'beyond' language; and of what use to us, historic/linguistic beings, is such a phenomenon? Croce's attempts to define 'taste' result then, in an extreme impoverishment of taste and a denial of art's cognitive import. In contradistinction, Della Volpe defines the tasks of criticism as firstly, to free itself from every type of mystificatory conception of taste, such as that offered by Idealists like Croce, and subsequently to formulate a truly scientific basis for aesthetics which would oppose and transcend the anti-rational aspects of Kant's conception of the autonomy and positivity of the aesthetic, whilst at the same time salvaging those rational aspects gleaned from the opposition between Classicism and Romanticism. What this amounts to is the search for a kind of taste which unites both 'feeling' and 'rationality' (precisely deemed impossible by Idealist aesthetics). The link lies in the concept of the 'concrete' or 'determinate abstraction' precisely through which, he argues, art is constituted.

It is precisely in this unity that Marx locates the real difficulty of the materialist in front of the general problem of art, in the 1857 'Introduction to the Critique of Political Economy'.[27] One must not, he reminds us, lose sight of the aspects of 'form' whilst examining the 'content', as most Marxist philosophers of art have done. (In this last note, Della Volpe is specifically critical of Zhdanov and socialist realism, but also of 'sociological' critics like Gramsci and Lukàcs.) Neither, however, must we concentrate purely on 'form' - a truly materialist aesthetic must carefully navigate between a crude sociology of content and an abstractly de-historicized formalism. In doing so Croce's stress on art as language, that,

'an image which is not expressed, which is not language ["parola"], even murmured to oneself, cannot exist',

can in fact be used to contradict the abstract mystical aspects of Croceanism itself, since it points towards the concrete rationality of art, its rootedness in the real material world, as rational historical discourse.[28]

This claim, which unites all the arts as different forms of concrete rationality, or intellectual/conceptual structures historically and culturally grounded in the real material world, able to be tested scientifically, whilst at the same time providing a critique of idealist metaphysical 'explanations' of art, summarizes the whole of Della Volpe's aesthetic project, later elaborated more fully in the *Critica del Gusto* (*Critique of Taste*).

Since the general epistemological characteristics of art (its synthesis of universality and particularity) are common to every other product of the understanding or reason, what needed to be further examined were the specific technico-semantic characteristics of the various arts, to which Della Volpe had referred in the 'Introduzione a una poetica aristotelica' ('Introduction to an Aristotelian Poetics') in the *Poetica del cinquecento* (*Sixteenth-century Poetics*), and was to pursue in the *Critica del Gusto* (*Critique of Taste*). The Kantian notion of the 'immediate pleasure' granted by aesthetic apperception can be re-elaborated in a materialist sense to verify the generic aspect of art, its 'realism' and hence the 'exemplarity' as rational-material synthesis, to which Marx alluded when he talked of the 'unattainable standard ... in a certain sense' of Greek art.

Della Volpe concludes by saying that the problem of aesthetic judgement cannot be posed or resolved by means of arguments which rely on hypostases, a priori or generic abstractions but on historical, functional and scientifically rigorous abstractions, which he terms 'determinate abstractions'. This notion of 'determinate abstraction' was one of the cornerstones of Della Volpe's critique of the a priori in the *Logica come scienza positiva* (*Logic as a Positive Science*), too large a topic to be handled adequately here.[29]

Filmic metaphor as filmic realism

In the essay which lends it title to the book, *Il Verosimile Filmico* (*Filmic Realism*), Della Volpe explores a suggestion of Pudovkin, that the content or script of a film, while it may offer a general idea to the director, is nevertheless different from, and powerless to dictate, its concrete form.[30] On this apparently simple observation rests an entire theory of the epistemological specificity of the 'filmic' image, as distinct from the 'literary', 'pictorial', 'musical' or other, image. Pudovkin, in identifying the peculiar 'plasticity' and 'concreteness' of the filmic image, highlights its direct capacity to function as metaphor or symbol, and hence a carrier of complex ideas about the real world. In a film, it is not so much the specific wording of the script which conveys meaning as the use to which the director puts this within a filmic image. In fact, he argues, it is the director's chief task to elaborate this filmic plasticity. Eisenstein, taking up Rudolph Arnheim's suggestion of the need for a 'new Laocöon', notes the difficulties in individuating the specificity of filmic metaphor in his comparison of painting and film:

28 G. Della Volpe, *op. cit.*, pp. 21-22.

29 see M. Montano, 'On the methodology of determinate abstraction', *Telos*, no. 7, Spring, 1971.

30 Pudovkin, *Film technique an film acting*, New York, 1949, p. 95.

31 S. Eisenstein, *Film Form*, trans. Jay Leyda, London, 1949, p. 60.

32 G. Della Volpe, *op. cit.*, pp. 40-43.

33 *ibid.*, p. 45.

34 *ibid.*, pp. 44-45.

In painting the form is born from the abstract elements of line and colour, whereas in the cinema the material concreteness of the image-frame as an element presents the greatest difficulty of [formal] elaboration.[31]

But Della Volpe argues that filmic metaphor is nevertheless possible not in terms of 'single frames' but conceived as a montage or juxtaposition sequence, and cites the juxtaposition of the images of the workers being killed and the slaughtered cattle in Eisenstein's *Strike* (1924) or the 'awakening lion' sequence in *Battleship Potemkin* (1925). In the first, the concrete, rational meaning of the filmic metaphor is the equation of the cold, methodical slaughter of the ox with the gunning down of the workers in the square; in the second the juxtaposition of the images of the 'awakening' stone lions, interspersed with images of the broadsides being fired from the battleship convey a sense of the awakening of the 'spirit' of rebellion in the Russian people ('even the stones rise up and shout' etc.). These images while being precise in the filmic sense are yet difficult to 'put into words' or translate into another expressive medium. These examples which reveal the concrete historical, discursive content of filmic metaphor serve to further highlight the crisis of the Crocean concept of 'cosmic intuition' which would see the 'image' as 'interior', 'ineffable' and removed from intellection.[32] Defining art as an 'a priori' synthesis of intuition and expression negates the aspect of 'technique' which in film is all the more evident. Croce himself saw that technique could not be separated from the artistic process but failed to acknowledge that it also played a determinate part in that process, thus forming part of the specific meaning of the artwork. Giovanni Gentile too, (the intellectual founder of Italian Fascism) in his theory of thought as the 'pure act', dissolves the epistemological positivity of technique in the a priori 'unity of opposites' by which he defines this 'act'.[33]

In contrast, Della Volpe argues for a conception of the filmic image as a concrete discourse which is constituted of determinate forms and ideas, just as the literary image is constituted. In this conception the traditional roles of 'form' and 'content' are reversed so that 'content' comes to refer to the concrete historical-discursive 'form' (its symbolic-communicative aspect) which constitutes the 'image'. The universality or objectivity of the artistic image is an attribute of the form of the concept, not of the image, and the term 'form' implies a determinate discriminate, rationally intelligible image. A 'form' which is 'unintelligible' is in fact a contradiction in terms, being a reversion to the neo-Platonic 'mystic oneness' of Plotinus, or the mystical unity of Schelling's 'mystic black night'. Moreover, the 'content' of the filmic/artistic must be none other than the concrete rationality of matter, of the 'sensible', historically actual.[34]

A further conclusion can be drawn from this that, as the form always directs us towards the content, so the content is nothing if it does not direct us towards the form, to the idea, for its full objectification or expression. The structural circularity of form and content which Della Volpe formulates here leads him to conclude that there can be no successful formal 'transcendence' of a content which is banal, academic or stereotypical, (and therefore 'untruthful') because the content cannot but influence the form: where there are only stereotypes and untruths, there can be no artistic (formal) value. Della Volpe notes that the reasons for this type of failure need not lie in the personal originality of the individual/artist and in his/her application of formal, technical norms, but rather:

Kenneth G. Hay

' ... in the non-dialectical use of expressive models, and that is of symbols or ideals, or ideas (forms), which have been historically (i.e. really) superseded or consumed'.[35]

35 *ibid.*, p. 46.

36 *ibid.*, pp. 49-50.

37 *ibid.*, pp. 48-49.

This, for Della Volpe, is the modern, post-Romantic problem of 'artistic originality'. Once the mystical and irrational definitions of form and content have been rejected, one is free to see that the dyad 'form-content' is none other than 'idea-matter' or 'empirical concept'. What differentiates artistic empirical concepts from empirical concepts in the normal or scientific sense is their different expressive means and semantic techniques, (*not* their rootedness in the material social and historical world), whereby film uses a dynamic-visual language, literature utilizes verbal symbols and images, painting adopts static-visual-'abstract' symbols and images, etc. The different 'species' of the genus 'art' (film, painting, literature, music etc.) can thus be conceptualized and their differing techniques analysed. Aristotle's definition of 'similitude' as a nexus linking 'distant and different things' such as happens in Philosophy and Science, proposes that metaphor (art) is thought (although not only thought) since it is in fact a 'transposition' (metaphor) from the genus to the species. An image, insofar as it is 'truthful' (i.e. coherent) will have a 'life-like' or realistic quality, even if the realism is 'impossible' in the Aristotelian definition (such as Eisenstein's stone lions 'awakening')[36]; i.e. it is preferable to have an 'impossible' but 'believable' image (i.e. successfully expressed) than an incredible (i.e. incoherent) but possible one. Aristotle argues that 'impossible' or 'unbelievable' images in art are 'errors' when directly connected to the technique of the artist, but not when they only have an 'accidental' relationship to this technique. Thus the notion of 'probability', as nexus of distant and distinct, as internal coherence, or internal rationality of the image takes on a central role as a constitutive condition of art, whether filmic, literary or pictorial etc.[37] Filmic probability is then the 'concrete form' or 'image' or 'filmic idea' which Pudovkin intended to distinguish from literary 'probability'. The distinction can be seen in the often crude attempts to 'transpose' one form (a novel) into another (a film) which lack artistic unity because they have been conceived in a form outside of the new medium. The literary idea, however brilliant, is to the director nothing more than 'abstract content' i.e. another material which has only an accidental relationship to the art of the director. This is a clear declaration, of the cognitive independence of different species of artistic form-making, which applies equally to the relationship of 'apparent' ('literary') and 'real' (concrete/material) content within the visual arts, (and music, etc.) which has, as Della Volpe remarked, waylaid most Marxist authors on art.

In *Pudovkin e l'attuale discussione estetica* (*Pudovkin and current aesthetic debate*) (1953) Della Volpe reiterates many of the arguments in *Il Verosimile Filmico* concerning Pudovkin's distinction of the different artistic 'genres', their differentiation by means of technique and the resultant difficulties of 'translating' from one genre to another. Giving fuller coverage of Pudovkin's opposition to both crude contentism and a self-conscious formalism (what Gramsci called 'calligraphism'), and G.M. Malenkov's critique of Engel's category of 'typicality' in art in the *Soviet Encyclopaedia*, Della Volpe finds that materialist aesthetics has reached a new phase. This constitutes a real advance on the work of Plekhanov and Lukàcs, because, while they remained 'outside' the work of art, caring little for artistic form or technique as such, and more or less indifferent to the epistemology

38 *ibid.*, p. 63.

39 *ibid.*, p. 65.

40 *ibid.*, p. 89.

41 *ibid.*, p. 91.

of art, preferring a typification of social contents in art, the work of Gramsci, Pudovkin and Malenkov reveals the work of art in its dialectic, and takes up the epistemological analysis of technical, structural or formal processes in art, and declares once and for all the indispensable contribution of intellect (concrete rationality) to the work, formerly thought to be 'ineffable' or 'pure imagination'.[38] Della Volpe sees in Malenkov's theory of the intellectuality of metaphor, an 'aesthetic neo-Aristotelianism' which parallels the adoption of Aristotelian criteria in discussions of metaphor in English criticism such as that of I.A. Richards, and counters aesthetic mysticism deriving ultimately from Platonism.[39]

In *Ideologia e film (Ideology and Film)* (1958), Della Volpe observes that:

> It is clear that it is not this or that ideology (or content) which counts artistically in the work of art, but whether there is a coherentand clear ideology which can contribute (when united with imagination) to create that ensemble of meanings and values without which there can be no universality of character and action - i.e. there can be no poetry.[40]

In *Situazione 58 (Situation 58)* Della Volpe characterizes black and white as the essential filmic medium, colour being the 'merely spectacular' preserve of 'second order' deluxe productions. This, conservative and clearly dated judgement contradicts the essential openness of Della Volpe's aesthetic, according to whose spirit, colour too should be seen to possess its own 'filmic language' capable of doing (thus 'saying') different things from black and white. Della Volpe returns to the problematic of specifically 'filmic language' in 'Postilla sul cinema e le arti figurativi', written after the *Critica del Gusto*. The more prolonged study enabled Della Volpe to return to the subject of filmic language with several additional observations. Firstly, that the two-dimensionality of film is merely a physical or 'contingent' characteristic of the medium and therefore 'external' to cinematographic work; whereas in painting, flatness is an intrinsic characteristic of the pictorial sign/value; Della Volpe also observes that the kind of spatial or artistic effects possible in painting, such as the use of straight lines and parallel walls of a room in a Giotto fresco to create an effect 'on the surface' do not lend themselves to cinematic treatment, because the film frame inevitably reproduces all three dimensions at once.[41] He then reiterates his view that colour in film is essentially a 'contamination' of filmic language which inevitably produces 'hybrid' effects. This seems to underestimate the capacity of a camera-angle to create specifically two-dimensional shots, such as, for instance the diagonal of black river/white snow in Huston's *The Dead* and the many 'still-life' shots in that film; Or the many instances of aerial shots or close-ups forming apparently 'abstract' patterns in films such as Eisenstein's *Battleship Potemkin*, Fritz Lang's *Metropolis*, Chaplin's *Hard Times*, or Léger's *Ballet Méchanique* - i.e. precisely those aspects of flatness, pattern and contrast which make the film-still into an effective two-dimensional 'film-poster'. A film-maker like David Lynch in *Blue Velvet* utilizes both high intensity colour and two-dimensionality in the opening shots of the white fence against clear blue sky to make essentially 'filmic' discourse, conveying a mood of heightened reality, and an uneasy blend of toytown and menace, essential to the film. Essentially two-dimensional close-up shots of ears, etc. continue this aspect throughout the film. On this point I disagree with what I see as Della Volpe's 'colour-blindness'.

With regards to the use of sound in movies, in keeping with his assertion of the essentiality of specific artistic discourse, Della Volpe's criticism of Kriss Marker's film *Joli mai* (1963) in *Sul cinema-vérité* (*On Cine-verite*) is that 'The microphone dominates too much' in other words that:

' ... the word prevails over the image, and that the words of the 'interviews' are insufficiently correlated to filmic images'.[42]

In order to be successful as film, *cinéma-vérité* should, according to Della Volpe, have a clear sociological content, a related ideological structure to give a precise meaning to that content, and thirdly, the image should predominate over the word, so that the latter is merely the starting point for a plastic elaboration.

Translatability in the *Critica Del Gusto*

The *Critica del Gusto* (*Critique of Taste*) is unquestionably Della Volpe's major contribution to the field of art theory. Its composition occupied him for around eleven years, from the first outlines of 1955 prior to its first publication in 1960, to the two subsequent reworkings of 1964 and 1966.[43] Initially, the work was titled *Critica materialistica* (*Materialist Criticism*) in answer to the need outlined in his earlier criticism, for a rigorously materialist aesthetic which would give full value to art's rational and historical foundation in concrete materiality.[44] Space here will allow me only to outline one or two themes.

Two fundamental ideas, developed from the *Verosimile Filmico*, (*Filmic Realism*) constitute the central core of the 'Critica del Gusto'. Namely, that any hierarchy of the arts in terms of expressive or artistic value is meaningless and theoretically redundant (the only tenable position being to recognize the legitimacy of the various arts as 'peacefully coexistent equals'); and secondly, in opposition to the Romantic-Idealist-Crocean concept of art as 'cosmic intuition', that Art be granted equal cognitive-epistemological status to History or Science, from which, in epistemological terms, it is distinguished only technically (i.e. semantically).

The claim for Art's equal cognitive value alongside Science and History, derives from the Aristotelian distinction between the genres of Poetry and History (between the expression of what is possible and what is merely actual).[45] If Aristotle's solution is no longer sufficient, and Poetry can no longer be seen as 'superior' to History (because even that which has happened could not have occurred if it were not possible), then the specific differentiating feature can only be individuated in the technical-semantic field - with the epistemological specificity of genres which this implies.

Since language is socially constructed, its form and structure are both socially functional and rational, rather than arbitrary or inherent; thus the dialectical relation of form and content is rooted in everyday language, and each branch of the arts must have its own special 'language' or expressive, technical-semantic sign-system, comprehensible only through the existence of a socially shared common logical language:

'The theory of the rational character of the sign, and the grounding of reason and meaning in ordinary, natural language, was developed definitively in the *Critica del Gusto*.'[46]

Taking his starting point from a suggestion of Goethe's that the 'pure and perfect

42 *ibid.*, p. 100.

43 cf. I. Ambrogio, in G. Della Volpe, *Opere*, vol. 6, p. 459; Both the English edition, (trans. Michael Caesar, London: N.L.B., 1978) and the definitive Italian edition in the *Opere*, annotated by I. Ambrogio, are based on the third Italian edition, published by Feltrinelli in 1966.

44 cf. I.Ambrogio, G. Della Volpe, *Opere*, vol. 6, p. 460; see *Opere*, vol. 5, p. 473.

45 Aristotle, *Poetics*, 1451b, 1ff.

46 J. Fraser, *An Introduction to the thought of Galvano Della Volpe*, Lawrence and Wishart, 1977, p. 239.

47 Goethe, 'Bertragungen', *Werke*, XV, Zürich, 1953, p. 1085; Della Volpe, *Opere* vol. 6, p. 156.

48 Della Volpe, p. 156.

49 Leopardi, 'Zibaldone', 2134-35, in *Tutte Le Opere*, ed. W. Binni, and E. Ghidetti, vol. I, p. 434 and vol. II, Florence, 1969, p. 564.

50 *ibid.*, 2134-35.

51 Della Volpe, *ibid.*, p, 168.

52 *ibid.*, p. 224.

53 V.I. Pudovkin, *Film Technique and film acting*, London, 1958, p. 116.

54 Della Volpe, *op. cit.*, p. 226.

content' of a poem is what remains when this is 'translated' into prose, Della Volpe develops his notion of 'critical paraphrase' as a means of identifying the logical core of the artwork.[47] This rational core remains after the 'dazzling exterior' of 'musicality' or rhythm (which pertain to the signifier and are thus external to the meaning as such) has been removed, and is thus synonymous with 'formed content' or poetic form in Della Volpe's analysis.[48] The criterion of translation must therefore only be fidelity to the letter of the poem. This is because even the literal translation is expressively and semantically a historical product so that fidelity to the objective spirit of the poem is at the same time fidelity to its subjective spirit. Poetry is thus always capable of being translated since it is this 'prosaic' aspect which alone corresponds to the discursivity of polysemic discourse. That which remains 'ineffable' or untranslatable is not the poem itself (as the Romantics would have us believe), but its euphony. For Leopardi, a perfect translation is one in which the author, translated from say French to German, is the same author in Italian or English, for which he maintains that poetry can only be translated by poets.[49] The difficulty or limitation in the accomplishment of this is due to specific semantic differences between languages, such that 'it is not always possible in all languages'.[50] The difference lies in what Saussure termed the linguistic value of the word as distinct from its meaning. The 'value' refers to the function of the word in the linguistic structure, and applies not only to words but also to grammatical entities and syntax. Since different languages have different syntactic structures and characteristic grammatical norms, it follows that a 'true' translation (i.e. one which captures the logical core of the work) will not necessarily mimic the syntactic structures of the original, and may need to depart quite far from them.[51] Ultimately the greatness of an author lies precisely in his/her ability to transcend these 'incidental' aspects of language - to become eminently 'translatable' in effect.

Cinema

For Della Volpe, cinema was not primarily a 'visual art' nor less a sub-species of painting. Della Volpe considered the two-dimensionality of film to be extrinsic and accidental to the nature of 'film-work'. The intrinsic feature of the frame (the basic film sign) is that it is a photographic reproduction of a three-dimensional real world, hence essentially documentary in character. Even montage is a counterpointing of frames in a sequence. A film is thus composed of 'edited photo-dynamic image-ideas'.[52] And colour, like the literary film score, was seen as a 'contamination' of the essential black and white essence. These filmic images, such as Eisenstein's stone lions in *Battleship Potemkin*, can be: 'reproduced in words only with difficulty', as Pudovkin observed.[53] Any attempt to 'describe' them, like the similar attempt to describe a dream, will be banal and impoverished by comparison with the vividness of the original, because they possess a superior 'optical-expressive force'[54] A similar banality would result in trying to 'translate' a peculiarly poetic image like that of the lion in Dante's *Inferno* (I, lines 47-48) into an essentially filmic image. In both, what should be kept in mind is the criterion of semantic difference, by which each expressive (art) form has its own autonomous range of expressive/formal/technical possibilities (and no others). For Della Volpe, the structural differences between the different artistic forms are semantic/technical and the philosophical justification of the different genres is the epistemological effect or import of their differing techniques - the fact that certain expressive aspects are not readily (if at all)

Kenneth G. Hay

translatable from one genre to another. Science does what science can; art practice follows different rules, but this is not to deny their epistemological contribution.

Conclusion

What are we to make of these insights in relation to artwork as research? By focusing on the problem of translatability between artistic genres (inter-semiotic translations) Della Volpe opens the way to a materialist understanding of the common material base of the arts and the sciences. The fact that there can never exist a full 'translation' across genres does not, however mean that the cognitive import of the arts cannot be grasped through words, and thus concrete knowledge, arrived at. Both the arts and sciences operate through the use of determinate abstractions through which the C-A-C' circle can be effectuated and concrete knowledge produced. His method offers insight into the interrelation of logic, meaning and aesthetics which are open-ended and flexible whilst being firmly rooted in historical analysis. As such it encourages a clear appreciation of the cognitive import of artistic practice as concrete abstraction, able to engage with, interpret and critique material, socio-historic and gendered experience. Its dialectical subtlety gives full cognizance of the specificity of artistic genres and procedures and of the complexity and limits to translatability operating between abstract ideas and form. It provides a useful methodological paradigm for framing the operational space required of a truly experimental research culture such as that required for a Ph.D. in Studio Practice. One sign of an active research culture is that curious people continue to seek after specific knowledges, building upon previous conceptions and methodologies to better understand 'what it is to be in the world'. It is a sign of life.

* This paper was originally given at a conference, 'The Enactment of Thinking', at the University of Plymouth's Exeter School of Arts & Design in July 2001. It presents the research in progress during a practice-based Ph.D., at UWE Bristol, using an overview of the findings to demonstrate the methodology and the integration of practice and theory. All illustrations are of the author's work, being examples of the practical element of the project.

A phenomenological study of the body and its representations in painting*

Karen Wallis

Abstract

This research originates in my practice as a painter and teacher of life drawing; and seeks to question whether the figurative nude in painting is unfinished business. Being a practising artist and not an academic, has influenced both my methodology and the relationship between practice and theory. Reading, visual practice, writing, and the analysis of other artists' work, all stimulate and inform each other; with the result that practice and theory have equal weight, neither being an illustration of the other. These dual concerns are not unified in one investigation but have developed as interdependent parallel strands. The practical element is a search to find strategies for painting the figurative nude, which can stimulate a sense of a corporeal body for the viewer. This theoretical investigation is an examination of the nature and structure of realism, its hermeneutical association with the viewer and its position in relation to the Kantian sublime.

My practice-based Ph.D. has grown out of my profession as a painter - and from teaching life drawing. As an artist, I was already asking questions that concerned the continuance of my discipline. For instance, why are life drawing and figurative painting being sidelined; and why does feminism find the outward appearance of the body difficult? Although artists informed by feminism are examining the body, both psychologically and physically, they do so from the inside. It is referred to through traces and absence - but is not allowed to be seen by others simply as it is.

When I began to use reading to support my work, further questions arose. How is it possible to make a painting of a nude which can avoid the 'male gaze'? Can a nude ever be portrayed to suggest the presence of an autonomous being - the naked body we all have as our vehicle for being in the world? If I undertook a research degree, would it offer the opportunity to make a radical investigation of life drawing - and to find out if the painted nude in the Western figurative tradition is unfinished business?

There has been a great deal of debate on methodology for Fine Art Ph.Ds. and how far we should follow existing methods set by other disciplines. I am primarily a practising artist, not an academic, and at the start of this research, knew little about established Ph.D. methodology. So I decided not to try to alter my artist's research to fit a methodology constructed for science or sociology. Instead, I looked for similarities in approach - in order to adapt an accepted methodology to my way of working. Here is a comparison between investigative drawing and scientific research. First I take the initial idea (or theory) and try it out on paper by making a drawing (as in testing an experiment). The image drawn (or result of the experiment) is analysed. Reflection on how to develop the image (or modify the theory) leads to further experimentation.

Figure 1. Artist and Model, *oil on canvas, 91.4 x 121.9 cm*

A sequence of studies on a progression, from artist with model to artist as model, was made while bearing this research process in mind, and became the first stage of an investigation informed by reading on phenomenology. In the search for a corporeal nude I explored the phenomenological experience of simultaneously seeing and being seen. As Merleau-Ponty said:

> It is ... not enough to say that the objective body belongs to the realm of 'for others', and my phenomenal body to that of 'for me', ... [they] exist in the same world, as is proved by my perception of an other who immediately brings me back to the condition of an object for him.[1]

In the next quotation from Merleau-Ponty - if you substitute the word 'practice' for 'philosophy' - his description of phenomenology might be an analogy for drawing from life:

> ... a philosophy for which the world is 'already there' before reflection begins - as an inalienable presence; and all its efforts are concentrated upon re-achieving a direct and primitive contact with the world ...[2]

Furthermore, he goes on to imply that art was ahead of philosophy by saying that:

1. Maurice Merleau-Ponty, *Phenomenology of Perception*, trans. Colin Smith, London: Routledge & Kegan Paul Ltd, 1962, p. 106 footnote.

2. Merleau-Ponty, *op. cit.*, Preface, p. vii.

3. *ibid.*, p. viii (Merleau-Ponty's emphasis).

Figure 2a. Study I, *charcoal on paper*

> ... the opinion of the responsible philosopher must be that *phenomenology can be practised and identified as a manner or style of thinking, that it existed as a movement before arriving at complete awareness of itself as a philosophy.*[3]

The analysis, of the series of drawings (fig. 2) and the subsequent painting (fig. 3), produced two main points for consideration. First, although using myself as the life model, the subject here is not self portraiture - it is about the relationship between one body and another. The phenomenological approach has caused a shift from a person or an object being the subject, to concentrate on the fluidity of the space between people or objects - where perceptions constantly shift and change. Second,

Karen Wallis

4. Maurice Blanchot, *The Space of Literature*, trans. Ann Smock , Lincoln: University of Nebraska Press, 1982, pp. 254-64.

Figure 2b. Study II, *charcoal on paper*

this approach also reveals the difference between physical perception and the manifestation of that perception - as a picture. The picture, which portrays the body, is seen as a separate object in its relationship to a viewer - who could be either the artist or a total stranger. Blanchot describes this as a fascinating image. He describes the situation when a tool is broken and loses its function, or a person dies and the living body becomes a corpse. It 'begins to resemble itself', taking on a 'cadaverous resemblance' and becomes an art object, removed from reality.[4] So in the light of these findings, my original aim - to portray a nude that could suggest the presence of an autonomous being - appeared to have serious problems. I therefore began an investigation into realism in painting.

A phenomenological study of the body and its representations in painting   81

Figure 2c. Study III, *charcoal on paper*

After examining many different concepts of realism, I was unable to find any
school of painting that communicated the sense of actuality that I was searching for.
Taking the phenomenological approach again, I began writing about individual
pictures as if I was drawing them - sometimes directly in front of the picture in a
gallery and sometimes from a reproduction in a book.

While looking at a painting, there occurs, on some occasions, an instant
recognition of actuality. There is a painting by Eric Fischl called *Grief,* it shows a
man on a rocky shore, in his underpants, dripping wet and holding a child of about

Karen Wallis

Figure 2d. Study IV, *charcoal on paper*

ten years. By Fischl's own admission, the painting technique is not good. I first saw it as a reproduction in a book and was not immediately impressed because of its poor quality as a painting. However, on taking a second look, I realized that the child the man is holding is dead - he has just pulled the body from the water. The impact was shocking - the vision of a parent's worst nightmare. The horror superseded all other aspects of the painting - including the doubtful technique. The effect is that I now find the painting extremely difficult to look at, because it is too real.

Usually a moment like this occurs to an individual but occasionally there is a collective reaction - for example, in the reception of Courbet's 'breakthrough pictures' during 1851. Courbet is described as the 'father of realism' but it is hard to understand the impact he had, unless the work is seen in context. For instance, his *Burial at Ornans* is the size of a history painting - 21 feet long - but the subject matter is not what was expected by the public at its first showing. They would have expected something like Couture's *Decadence of Rome* - which was shown in the same year, and now hangs close by at the Musée d'Orsay. The public were not only unaccustomed to the relationship between its size and subject matter, they also found the figures portrayed were not clear cut classical stereotypes but recognizable as contemporary people - including some of indeterminate social background. The public reaction to Courbet's *Burial at Ornans* was that this was realism.

A phenomenological study of the body and its representations in painting   83

Figure 3. Mother and daughter I, *oil on canvas, 63.5 x 76 cm*

This incident and others like it - the reception of Manet's *Olympia,* for instance - show that realism, in the context of this research, is not a style of painting but an event. By reading Gadamer, it became clear that an event of realism is the viewer's hermeneutical interaction with a particular image - an image capable of touching their own existence.

An example related to my own work proved to be a key moment in the development of the practical strand of my research. While making my next series of drawings, a friend had a particular reaction to a study of my naked body reflected in a mirror over the bathroom basin (fig. 4). He said that when he 'looked in the mirror' he expected to see himself - but instead, he saw me.

To allow the nude to be seen afresh, outside its traditional readings, it is necessary to create a situation similar in its reception to that of *Burial at Ornans.* This means provoking an effect in the viewer - by applying a knowledge of hermeneutics to the phenomenological practice. It was at this stage that I wondered if an event of realism was connected to the Kantian sublime - being the effect on us of our perception, rather than the act of perception itself - as when we see something as beautiful.

The main objectives of my research were now established. In fine art practice I would develop strategies for making figurative paintings of the nude which might stimulate, in the viewer, a sense of a 'real' body. This would be supported by an

Karen Wallis

Figure 4 Bathroom study, *charcoal on paper*

examination of representations of the body; in particular those works that stimulate a sense of a real existence, by relating the body portrayed to the world of the viewer. In the theoretical strand, I would investigate the nature of realism as an event for the viewer, through a study of phenomenology, hermeneutics and alterity. Although closely connected, the two strands of practice and theory were not completely integrated but ran in parallel - each informing and stimulating the other.

The issue of appropriate methodology was also becoming clearer. My research was combining a phenomenological approach, as the principal method in both practice and theory; but with philosophical, historical, descriptive, and experimental

5. Janet Wolff, *Resident Alien*, Cambridge: Polity Press, 1995, p. 45.

6. Walter Benjamin, *Understanding Brecht*, trans. Anna Bostock, London: Verso, 1983, pp. 15-22.

elements also evident. However, the use, not only of my own painting but also my own body, raises the question of subjectivity - in a discipline that is traditionally objective. This project should be regarded as reflexive practice, seen in a context indicated by Janet Wolff's observations on Walter Benjamin's use of memoir:

> the interplay of the autobiographical and the critical in his work accords well with contemporary tendencies to integrate these two modes of writing; at the same time, the analytics of the concrete are very much in tune with the current rejection of abstract theory and the desire for specificity.[5]

In fact, my position as both 'subject' and 'object' is quite straightforward. By taking on the roles of both artist *and* model (as the *body* that simultaneously sees and is seen) I am able to affirm both points of view. In so doing, I take on the additional role of the researcher who deconstructs each position through a process of affirmation. Given that we are all flawed in our subjectivity, it is better to affirm the personal involvement in a situation and then use what that reveals.

***

The concept of an event of realism reveals the importance of the situation in which the picture is seen. To create such a situation requires either a change of context or a disruption in the normal method of presenting work. Walter Benjamin's account of Brecht's epic theatre[6] is comparable to an event of realism and offers a potential method for disrupting the hermeneutical play between picture and viewer. To adopt Brechtian strategies: the audience should be 'relaxed', aware of who and where they are; the 'story' must be unsensational; there should be an 'untragic hero' used as a character who observes the action; 'interruptions' in the action will 'dis-cover' - or alienate - the conditions represented; 'quotable gestures' will cause interruptions; the play should be 'didactic' as an experience, rather than a thrilling sensation; 'the actor' not only shows the event, but reveals herself or himself as a player; by using a 'dais', rather than a stage, the distance between the action and the audience is reduced. All these qualities make epic theatre less dramatic than classical theatre - but the effects are more radical. This can be seen as an analogy to an event of realism.

To put Brechtian principles into practice, I decided to see if the aura of the painted nude could be disrupted by presenting 'art' in the 'wrong' place. Rather than disrupt the art space with a ready-made object - I would try to disrupt the ordinary world with an art object. The first attempt was in work exhibited in the Faculty of Art, Media and Design at UWE. *Triptych* was installed in a corridor between the porter's office and students' union shop. It consisted of three paintings, originating from the bathroom study mentioned above, each in a frame with narrow mirrors hinged on either side and a long mirror on the wall opposite. The mirrors were positioned so that the viewer would see their own reflection when they were standing in front of the painting. Two more works, *Hand Towel* and *Wash Basin* (fig. 5), were installed in the Ladies' toilets at the end of the adjoining corridor. These were paintings on paper mounted on mirrors - so that the image obstructed the viewer's reflection in the mirror.

Feedback showed that the venues and manner of installation did influence the viewer's reaction to the painted nude. The images in the toilet were regarded as

Karen Wallis

Figure 5. Wash Basin, *installation – oil on paper mounted on mirror*

friendly, while the work in the corridor was felt to be uncomfortable. This appeared to be influenced by what the images asked of the viewer; in the toilet I put myself into the space the viewer was occupying - allowing myself to appear vulnerable; whereas in the corridor I was asking the viewers to come into my space in the picture - to make themselves naked with me.

Brectian strategies appeared to work; but the question remained as to whether the event of realism still had a connection to the sublime? Kant's concept of the

Figure 6. Triptych, *installation – oil paintings, mirror and computer prints*

sublime is essentially uplifting and transports one out of one's existence - like the absorption in Aristotelian tragedy - which is precisely what Brecht seeks to avoid. The viewer who senses realism clearly remains in touch with their world - as an 'interested' audience. In fact the sensation of the real is closer to the experience of the tragic in actuality, than tragedy in the theatre. Therefore it is uncertain where the sensation of the real is situated, in relation to the sublime.

Leaving this problem on one side for the moment, I returned to my practical work, to develop the exploration into the context in which the nude was seen - and to try to push the research forward, through feedback from visitors to an exhibition. In *now you see me ...* at the Black Swan Guild, in Frome, the work was shown in three different sites: abstract photographic computer prints of acceptable nudity in the Café; site specific paintings on mirrors in the Ladies' toilet; and another version of *Triptych* - with more explicit photographic computer prints - in the Gallery (fig. 6).

I hoped to use the access to the general public to gather feedback from a wider range of opinion than had been possible at UWE. The opportunity to comment was offered, anonymously if wished - either by posting written comments in a box, by e-mail, or by leaving a contact number to arrange an interview. Free workshops at the exhibition were offered to local secondary schools, colleges, WI's, U3A, the Round Table, and a naturist group. About 32 people commented in various ways through the comments box system and 25 people took part in four workshops - an A level group, a U3A art class, three men, and a postgraduate group from UWE. Although

Karen Wallis

Figure 7. Renoir in the bathroom, *installation – oil painting and mirror*

the discussions in the workshops were interesting and varied, I was disappointed with the take-up - out of 68 groups and institutions, only two took up the offer and so two more were arranged through personal contact. The written comments had their limitations too - they tended to be enthusiastic rather than positively critical. Also people with art education were inclined to place themselves in schools of thought - in favour of either painting, or installation with photography - but not both. Occasionally however, interesting remarks were unintentionally overheard; as when a small child pointed out the 'rude pictures' to her mother in the Ladies' toilets, or when a mother entered the Gallery with her children and left hurriedly saying 'too much flesh'.

The absence of comment, and lack of interest in workshops, is as telling as the comments collected. At a seminar after the exhibition, to report on the results, my methods of gaining feedback were called into question. My reply was that the situation of an art exhibition is not suited to the sort of sampling for information used by the social sciences, for instance. Although surveillance would have been interesting if unethical, it seemed better to look at the reasons for not obtaining comment and to work from there. I was beginning to realize that the solutions I was looking for, appeared to exist in between, or just outside, established ideas or concepts. Not only is an event of realism hard to place, but reaction to images of the nude are not quantifiable.

A phenomenological study of the body and its representations in painting   89

Figure 8. Lipstick, *installation – oil painting, mirror and muslin curtain*

Persevering with the practice, I tried another strategy in the next project. The *In House* group are six artists who install site-specific and site-sensitive work in domestic environments. In 1999, the group found two households willing to have work installed in their homes - sometimes directly on the wall - for a two-week exhibition called *In House Twice*. The opportunity to work with the householders shifted the context for my work from the place to the person. Consultation with the women in each house, during the production process, brought a portrait element into my images of the nude.

The couple at one house were naturists and their bathroom had a definite celebratory feel. I made a painting based on one of their postcards - a Renoir nude drying her foot - but portrayed myself, rather than the woman of the family, getting into their bath, and installed the painting on a mirror (fig. 7).

At the other house, the mother, just turned forty, was exploring her femininity by experimenting with lipstick for the first time. She had a row of lipsticks in a bathroom alcove, which begged to become a shrine. Using the painting on mirror technique again, I portrayed myself nude putting on lipstick and hung it in the alcove (fig. 8). In the same house, I also did a life-size charcoal drawing of myself and installed it on a landing 'looking out of the window'.

Despite using my own body, these images reflect the personalities of the woman in each house. The work has become a form of performance, with distinct similarities to Brecht's epic theatre.

Figure 9. Jackpot Sarong, *coloured chalks on paper*

The *In House* exhibition was installed without labels and situated throughout both the houses, in amongst the families' belongings. There were no clear boundaries between the art and 'real life'. The exhibition was open to the general public, by appointment, and visitors to both houses had a good variety of reactions. They tended to enjoy the permission to be nosy; but while some liked having to 'hunt the art', others found it frustrating. Subsequently we produced a book of the exhibition. By making the book start at both ends - one for each house - and putting our artists' statement in the middle, we managed to retain an element of hide-and-seek. For me, this blurring of boundaries is appropriate. It reflects my research - the shifting positions that occur between one thing and another, and between one idea and another. All answers appear to be just out of reach - or out of sight.

At this stage in the project the results are inconclusive. In the theoretical strand, it has not been possible to define the exact structure of an event of realism. It seems to occur somewhere between self-consciousness and the unconscious, between remembrance and involuntary memory, between ironic reflection and spontaneous thought, and between the subjective and objective.

The practical work has moved on another stage but, although the strategies appear to work, I now find myself far removed from both the gallery space and life room, where the research started. At a residency in a clothes shop, I had the opportunity to portray my body, untransformed and visible - implied rather than actual nakedness - inside clothes usually shown on a size 10 model (fig. 9). The project was highly successful in terms of presenting an acceptable body to the widest audience - providing good opportunities for conversation and feedback. It did bring the issue of the appearance of the ordinary body to the attention of the general public but I was clothed rather than naked and a long way from a gallery. The issues that were presenting themselves - reality in fashion and advertising - were moving away from my original investigation.

The question remains of whether it is possible, through my painting practice, to readdress the issue of the painted nude in its traditional context. An exhibition in a gallery uses an art-educated vocabulary, where images of the body are seen in the context of visual culture - both past and present. The Ph.D. research has shown that an event of realism is successful when the work is site specific and in a non-gallery situation. The challenge remains, to get back inside a designated art space and see if the same strategies will work in that context.

Karen Wallis

The Materiality of Text and Body in Painting and Darkroom Processes: an investigation through practice

Deborah Robinson

Abstract

The written component of my research charts the repositioning of a painting practice through the making of three discrete bodies of work. Each is accompanied by a 'practice text' based on notes made whilst making the work, the writing of these texts allowed me to discover the theoretical issues in the work, these then generated another layer of writing that discusses historical and theoretical issues in context. Inscriptions is an example of practice-based writing produced during the early stages of the research. At this point I was investigating the historical tradition from which my practice as an abstract painter stemmed. To do this I immersed myself in processes and techniques that originated with the American painter Helen Frankenthaler (b. 1928). Frankenthaler's working methods were marginalized by the canon whose values reflected a gender bias in favour of male creativity. As a woman painter I believed that these ideologies still had the power to determine how I responded to the medium of paint. I therefore applied a 'deconstructive' method to practice as an attempt to unearth the remnants of a historical framework that, to some degree, determines how the medium is conceptualized. The work I made was produced out of the tension of bringing together ideas taken from opposing paradigms, modernism and feminism. The modernist ideas were located in the medium itself, whereas feminist ideas taken from psychoanalytic and philosophic theory were accessed in textual form which was, during the process of making, responded to as a medium. Historically, within the critical framework of Abstract Expressionism, response to the medium was sexualized in accord with male values and sexuality. However, this problem can be located as part of a far broader discussion within a philosophical and psychoanalytic frame. Here, recent work by feminist thinkers such as Luce Irigaray, Judith Butler, Vicki Kirby, and Elizabeth Grosz provide a sustained inquiry into the sexualization of matter. Their ideas can be productively related to abstract painting which is, at its most basic, the organization of matter.

In making my own body of work *Inscriptions* I experimented with the text 'Inscriptions from Inside the Shell', by the artist and psychoanalytic theorist Bracha Lichtenberg Ettinger. In this text Ettinger theorizes a specifically feminine space, one that requires a very different understanding to pictorial space as it has been framed within modernism. The following text reflects the findings of this practice-based method.

Inscriptions: a description of a practice-based method

Initially I was drawn to Ettinger's writing in that it seemed to connect with, and release, a series of thoughts and feelings, which were deeply personal. However, a desire to immerse myself in an intimate relation to text was intermittently interrupted by confrontation with my own lack of theoretical understanding - the knowledge that certain words and meanings were closed/distant. At that point there seemed to be a choice between developing an academic understanding of Ettinger's theoretical position through either further reading or practice.

I decided to make some work and therefore what follows is an attempt to trace the way in which a dialectical reading of text influenced the process of making. First, I want to describe the lure of the written word, the sense of complete uninterrupted moments of connectedness to images evoked through text. To have this relation with the text it was necessary to glance at words, avoiding being caught in its logical structure. Responded to in this way, the text released images or sensations, which never became entirely focused or complete, but were nonetheless intense. Whilst making the work, I attempted to amplify, and give form to, partial images released by words - these were not necessarily visual, but seated in bodily sensations. This could be the way in which the tongue experiences the mouth, the vulnerability of liquid, or being muffled within a coil. These are images that shift into series of other images. I am wary that exposing these fleeting sensations to the process of describing through words will fix them in a way which is not what they are. During the process of making work, there is a chance element of finding some physical quality in the mediums which has an association with images released by the text.

What I have described appears to be an experience of being pulled under, being caught in some deep current of subjective response. It also carries sexual connotations. I have found, however, it is not possible to become wholly immersed in this way with this particular text. There is another response, a reaction that interferes almost all of the time.

At that same moment of subjective response, the words seem to exist in some distant arid space. It is therefore beyond my ability to make rational sense of what is written. The text is, in part, closed. I cannot respond to this reflection of myself as non-comprehending with neutrality. Irritability and frustration seem the basis of that part of my relationship to text, paralleling other patterns of unresolved relationships in which there is a compelling tendency to be caught up in a negative and boundaryless way. I am trying to explain something that is quite obsessive, a continued returning to the text/object with an unclear purpose. This returning to is 'acted out' in the systematic method of working employed in these paintings.

Irritability and frustration resulted in my first tearing at, fragmenting the text in order to extricate that part of it which I needed. Fragmentation perhaps suggests breaking or even shattering of the object/text and is therefore not entirely accurate. Even at the early stages of working, order was important - the way in which I tore the words, creating strips of paper following the lines of the text, involved a consideration of the formal order of the text. This process became gradually more systematic, even a ritualized process whereby text could be read/related to and then incorporated into the paintings. I began to use scissors to cut quantities of text, the act of cutting became the act of reading. Many incidental views of words were gleaned, the progress through the text slowed down. Steadied by cutting along each line I could see the words from a variety of viewpoints. This multiplicity of viewpoints, continuous contact with text at unplanned moments is a way of understanding its meaning, both in a subjective and rational sense.

In this series of work I have used colour-photocopied text. The origin of this method of working was accidental. I took a copy of the text 'Inscriptions from Inside the Shell' on a machine previously set by another user. Rather than the black and white copy I expected, what emerged were white words against an incredibly beautiful

Deborah Robinson

rich background, deep dull green with what seemed to be a shadow across part. The words were embedded in background colour that was shifting and watery. Reading is sometimes a confrontation with the harsh positive/negative relation of black to white. There was a way in which the coloured text allowed me to be spatially behind the words, that the act of reading was like breaking the surface after diving. I made the first of this series of paintings from this particular text which seemed mysterious in that, despite many experiments, I've never managed to repeat this particular effect.

This is what I remember of making the first painting. I cut the text quite carefully into thin strips and formed one into a spiral. Then I placed this text/form against the palm of my hand. In this position I could examine text in a new, vulnerable form. I felt it as a small animal moving slightly. It also felt a little like a Japanese fortune-telling fish, the paper would quite suddenly move, flip or uncoil. As a three-dimensional form, coloured text revealed the whiteness of its underside. In order to connect the two sides a colour highlighter was used to fill in the white with a luminous pink. The double-sided colours related and pink had nearly the right association with inner/body shell like forms that were suggested by the text.

I positioned the spirals of text across the surface of my paintings, in lines of five and positioned by eye, each was held by transparent glue. This presented a problem, they looked 'stuck on', and it was necessary to establish a figure/ground relationship within the picture surface. The solution was to pour liquid wax into each coil. After several experiments I found that by doing this I could forge a connection between the flat pictorial surface and the three-dimensional text.

At this point, I perceived the text as line upon line of holes, each plugged by wax. Words within the centre of each spiral were totally covered, muffled, gagged, lost to view. The luminous pink interior became dispersed, crystalline.

The act of pouring the liquid wax required a studied balance between control and uncontrol. I noticed that the wax flowed outwards from the spiral shapes holding its own liquid form against the surface of the muslin (this could only be achieved when the wax was close to setting, if too hot it seeped through the material). The pouring of the wax became a systematic act, which involved a high degree of artifice. By this I mean that, in order to make what looks like accidental effects, a high degree of technical control is necessary. This is in line with abstract expressionist working methods where what appears to be accident is very knowingly arrived at. I wanted an appearance of flow, liquid freely finding its form, but in reality this was achieved by tight technical control whilst carrying out a systematic repetitive task.

Whilst looking at this work again this afternoon I noticed that initially the words were positioned with small regard for the reader/viewer. Some of the first spirals were upside down. However, as the work progressed the text was placed with more care so that strings of words were visible.

These words are only accessible to the viewer from a crouching position beneath the work; it is necessary to be close and looking upwards. If the work were sited horizontally, rather than against the wall, it would obviously make reading the text easier. However, I shall wall hang the work because I want the work to be read within the context of painting as simultaneously the text 'jams' a purely experiential reading.

Reference

Lictenberg Ettinger, Bracha, 'Inscription from Inside the Shell', in *Inside the Visible; an elliptical traverse of twentieth-century art in, and from the feminine*, ed. Catherine De Zegher, Cambridge, Mass. and London: MIT Press, 1996, p. 106.

1   Presently archived at the British Museum London, as the only remaining textual evidence of/from Echo's estate. This documentation being separate from a single dried lily - presumably from the 'pool' [Ovid, *Metamorphosis III*, pp. 391-429] along the banks of which Narcissus was known to 'hang out'.

The Letter, or *Eurydice's last despatch to Echo*.[1] (A play in one act.)

Partou Zia

' *As a matter of fact, my dear Simmias and Cebes,*' *said Socrates,* '*it is proved already, if you will combine this last argument with the one about which we agreed before, that every living thing comes from the dead. If the soul exists before birth, and if when it proceeds towards life and is born it must be born from death or the dead state, surely it must also exist after death, if it must be born again. So the point which you mention has been proved already. But in spite of this I believe that you and Simmias would like to spin out the discussion still more; you are afraid, as children are, that when the soul emerges from the body the wind may really puff it away and scatter it, especially when a person does not die on a calm day but with a gale blowing.*' *[Plato, The Phaedo, 76B-77B]*

The Players: British Museum Archivist: female
                  Eurydice
                  Echo
                  Chorus: 1 & 2 'Archivists' [female voices]
                  Cleaner: female
                  Other Voices [overheard female and male voices/conversations]

The stage lights up onto a large archival room [arkheion]. The play takes place entirely on this one set: the British Museum archive rooms, situated in the basement of the museum (London). There are high-stacked shelving systems with archival boxes and wooden drawers on all sides of the stage, which with the help of visual projections or trompe l'oeil effects give the illusion of a very long official room. Some special-effect lighting to create a dusty, and gloaming atmosphere will help to convey the idea of a place of work which has been the locus for housing ancient artefacts and texts since the early days of the museum's own history, in the nineteenth century. In the middle of the stage there are a couple of solid old wooden tables strewn with ancient manuscripts, scrolls of parchment, and several Solander boxes, some of which are open with their contents spilling out on to the table. There are some high-set windows, grilled for security purposes that probably open out to the backyard/parking lot of the museum. Every now and then car tyres or the lower part of a passer-by (museum worker) is seen through the murky glass panes of these window openings. A solid grey door to the left of the stage, and a 'Fire Exit' situated to the back of the stage. There is an old-fashioned wall clock just above the grey entrance, and a coffee machine set on top of a cabinet is situated to the left of the door. A background of 'museum' noises and sounds, such as doors being opened and shut, footsteps in the corridors outside of the staged room, a goods trolley being pulled or pushed, with accompanied snippets of conversation, and guided tour loudspeakers instructing the visitors to the museum on the floor above, (etc.) are audible throughout the performance. The young female archival research assistant is the central figure on stage, and the play opens with her sifting through the stacks of Solander boxes on the table. She hums and mutters to herself as she works. The chorus are also on stage, but somehow only lit or seen when they actually speak. They are also archivists, seen moving in and out of the rows of shelving, or sometimes bringing a box to the table to examine.

Both Eurydice and Echo are seen at either end of the stage, dressed in archaic Greek mantle - staged as actual holograms, or live actresses, lit in an unearthly light, as though they are ghosts or visions. Eurydice carries a golden harp, and there is a dead snake at her foot. Echo sits on a mossy boulder, playing with a couple of freshly picked lilies; her speech is always broadcast a few seconds after she opens her mouth to speak. Neither of them need remain static, they can move or improvise dance steps, etc. where and if the production sees fit. The crackling of paper and sounds of parchment being unfolded or moved about fill the pauses in speech.

[*Curtain up very slowly*]

Act [the] One

Archivist: [*Singing to herself, and moving to her own humming*] You say potato, I say potato; potato, potato, let's call the whole thing off, etc. - Well, well, well, [*She stops and half turning to the audience unfurls a large codex manuscript*] and didn't Mr. Haystoric say emphatically that there was no known record from the classical period. [*She stammers in Greek*] My - EKHO, My - Echo, of course, a letter to Echo; [*She begins to decipher in stammering Greek as she translates into English*] - 'My dear Echo, By the time you receive this note I may be too far deep to answer any return of post that may arrive here.' [*As the Archivist reads, she takes up her pencil and sitting down begins to translate the manuscript. The light shifts from her on to Eurydice, who reads the text in her own voice*]

Other Voices: Yeah, I know! You want room 2B - first right.

Eurydice: Here all is a perfection of dense hues. Layers of dark earth-fired browns, and the dawns are a purple-stained streak that settles all the morning, lining the hollows, until the early dusk when the glimmer of a forlorn hope winks cadmium orange, after which momentary relief all is a uniform blue; darkest imaginable, and coldest, strangest of blues. Well that is where I am: here, in the underworld of all worlds. And no, I am not alone. There are many others - dark companions of this interterrestrial zone. Here time defies Time, and thought defies thinking. I want for nothing but to know the name of things again. To remember what the real meaning of things and words are. Nothing ever sounds right in my mouth any more, that's why I've taken to sighing and breathing with a heavy longing in my voice. Sometimes I hum a tune, and even watch as my fingers tap a rhythm, or feel my head sway from side to side. But I have not actually given voice to song for a long time. I was the daughter of song and melody. I was born to find the true words for feelings and memories to which people could tap their feet and move their bodies, in flirtation and joy. But now all I do is distrust the few names and words that still remain in my mouth.

Echo: Their bodies distrust the names in my mouth.

Chorus 1:   What is it that hurts?
               Pride - said the blackbird, languid and at home.

Eurydice: There are no rules here.

Echo: [*Holding the Letter*] We speak. - Don't get me wrong we speak. - Not always to each other - but at least there are voices all about.

Other Voices: Please follow me, - this way to the Roman Copies. No touching, sir! Thank you.

Eurydice: The walls are transparent and yet impenetrable. How I long for the light; to see the fresh shy-green of spring leaves. And I forget how the wind-feathered steps of a bird sounds.

Echo: I breathe only the past; the present has never arrived.

Eurydice: And Time is in such dishevelled threads that I barely know how it all hangs together. All day we stitch and sew the pieces of history long ago muddied by Time's misadventures.

Echo: The shadows of our needles dance to a voice-less tune.

Chorus 2:   A stitch in time is only more time and Time is stitch in time enshrined.

Echo: How I wish to break this yarn of half-truths. - History will never know what Time forgot.

Other Voices: Well that's what they told me, no fibbing. He's going, you'll be relieved to know. But promise to keep it close to your chest, there's a good girl. See you later then.

Chorus 1 & 2: Truth is a lie and lies are only stories told with aplomb.

Eurydice: I need your help my dear Echo. Even if you were to only read this letter out loud to the dear shining woods and valleys, someone or thing is bound to hear my story, resonate against your tongue-less voice. My cloth of life is no more a shining mantle, now stained by the silent gravity of deceit. My songs are gone, stolen, given new titles and sung in the base-timbre of a youthful bard. I would have happily shared my mysteries, my poetry, my voice even, but he was impatient, and foolish. That shambles with the venomous bite was a masquerade worthy of the travelling circus. Everyone knows that snakes don't bite women. As we know my dear E, Mr Ovid is a gullible old fool to believe all he hears. As you know very well not everything is what it sounds.

Echo: Not what it sounds! - Mr Ovid you know not! - What sounds?

Chorus 1:   Mr Ovid conceives Eurydice as Tragic!
               Mr Ovid says Echo is somewhat Comic!

Archivist: [As she reads and transcribes, the shadowy figures of the Chorus move about on the stage; doors slam and a general unease is generated] 'Did you know there are no doors here? A nightmare place; no privacy! Always some shadow mobile and curled just behind me, or espied hidden against the corner of a wall.'

Echo: I am exhausted with trying to keep myself to myself. - The public life is a perilous venom to the soul.

Other Voices: No, No, No, No! This way! Push it towards me! That's it, a bit more, and in we go.

Eurydice: By the way are you still courting and calling him? Is that vain youth still searching for a glimpse of his puerile visage fleeting the eddying waters?

Echo: Vain youth fleeting still calling his visage in the eddying waters.

Chorus 1 & 2: How the wind howls
               How the river gurgles
               How the clouds dance
               How the earth breaks
               Listen! - All is sound sounding out sound.

Eurydice: If only you would write him a message, or sing him a song that could be heard. Send him word. Paint your face on a mirror and have those sycophant nymphs hold it under water. Do anything but repeat your call.

Echo   Repeat your call back to him. - Echo not the self-ruinous shadow part of this phantom boy. - Forever afloat a voice that cannot be wedded to a body is not.

Eurydice: What madness! You must stop trying to make sense. Sing! Hum a tune! Dance, and stamp the ground! Play an instrument! But don't speak a voiceless speech. Huh! And who am I to be giving advice?! Here I am my voice and my body both cancelled out, given in love to my beloved O, who roams the dank dales and is celebrated as the peerless bard, winning hearts high and low.

Echo: O! My peerless O! - Who roams in my heart - Your call cancels me high and low.

Chorus 1& 2:   And when the serpent spoke we hissed in disbelief
And when Orpheus turned to look we knew his deliberation
And when she wept silent resignation we knew her as sacrifice.

Eurydice: We are to blame. I myself am the accomplice that strummed my instrument of fate. Strange, dear Echo, how both of us are made mute for our respective talents: you for your gift of improvised speech; and I for my gift of poetic mysteries.

Echo: In the name of all that is mysterious - written on the gateway to love we are muted in the hinge of truth.

Other Voices: Well, yes, yes of course, we all agree on the main issue, but there are other logistics to be considered here; don't you think?

Eurydice: It is up to you now, Echo. You are in the world. Go and speak my truth in resonance ten-hundred-fold. Find a high and deep place by a stony wall, stand proud and read my letter out loud. Let us become embedded in the mortar that seals the cobbled way, each footfall sounding a harbinger of warning to the intrepid traveller on the way to Love.

Chorus 2:   A monument to memory
A stone hewn to patience
A breath clamouring to hope.

Archivist: [*Walking absent-mindedly towards the coffee machine placed near the door*] 'The promise of total unity, no longer alone but one graduated to two, acting as one. She binds her name in love-woven forgetfulness.' [*She sips her coffee*] 'And how delicious to melt into the prospect of two opposites making one harmony!'

Chorus 2:   Syzygy does not recognize injustice to the other.

Chorus 1:   You echo your echo and echo is your echo, back.

Eurydice: I have no revenge in mind. There is a small spider near my head, spinning a dark glimmering architecture of hope. Sometimes in this light-bereft place I hear the spider whisper: 'Where does betrayal begin, and protection end?'

Partou Zia

Echo:	And in the end I recognize that whisper, telling me that light is my protection to the end. - Small hope.
Eurydice:	You know Echo, perhaps after all it is you who is the wisest of us all. Your unheard syllable is the declamation of other lives that are forever lost in the dispossessed records of everything that is mis-spelt, and unnamed. Your duplicating muteness that is rarely silent hums the alliteration of those archival gaps.
Chorus 1& 2:	Why turn Knowing each turn brings another Fall? Irreparable Irredeemable Irresponsible Why turn? Don't!
Echo:	Bring each knowing to another. - Turn: Why don't you?
Eurydice:	No, No! Mr Rilke! It is not Orpheus, that lover of mine, that bright god who bears your stigmata of the 'Infinite trace'. My absence IS the Mystery. Go ask Eumolpus, ask him: 'Who is the true bearer of Mysteries?' He will tell you of a silent girl whose sacred name was whispered in the quiet of the dawn by her ancient grandmother. A wise whisper in the fold of her ear, Eurydice was her given name: from mother to mother she held the secret in her soft newborn ear. As did Electra, Antigone, Io, Echo, Andromeda, and Cybele, - herself Mother of the Gods. Yes! Mr. Rilke! I am the lost god, the long-forgotten song, and the yearned-for poem who is sought by every poet born, dying, dead or alive.
Chorus 1 & 2:	OSY ∧∧∧ OSYA ∧∧∧ OSY Beware! Keep the serpent away Beware! Sing the serpent away OSY ∧∧∧ OSYA ∧∧∧ OSY As you walk the Ink of the night OSY ∧∧∧ OSYA ∧∧∧ OSY.
Eurydice:	My long-suffering mute one, my dear friend. If only you had listened to me and taken up writing or even drawing and painting, instead of improvised oration, and mimicry. On the wings of your breath that boy's ego has bellowed to over-size bursting point. Please take heed, and start practising the word; inscribe it, draw and mould it in the earth, but for my sake, no more emptiness in place of emptiness. Let the unspoken remain unspoken. Do not replicate the other's fantasy as assistant to your own destruction. Stop and think!

Echo:	No more mute muteness no more she.
Other Voices:	Please note the Museum will be shutting in ten minutes. All visitors please make your way to the two exits as soon as possible. Please note the Museum will be [...]
Archivist:	[*Looking up at the clock, and anxiously scribbling her transcription*] 'Here I must sign away my last word. Except for my hope enfolded in the fullness of this letter, I have little to look forward to but that I dissolve into the dark anonymity of a bogus tale. Let the birds always remember that it was I who gave them their sweet-syntactic strangeness and zest of song. Let the birds sing every syllable of my name, and lament the treachery of human love.'
Echo:	Let love's name enfolding in the dark letter of your name in every bird-song to hear that love is the strange human song to hope for you to hear love.
Chorus 1 & 2:	I sign *my* name in *your* name in *my* name in *your* name is *my* name is *your* name a name in *her* name. [*Repeated into a faded sound of name, name, name, etc.*]
Archivist:	Oh No! I'll miss the bus! [*The Archivist looks up at the clock, and suddenly drops the manuscript. Grabbing her coat and bag she hurries out*]
	[*As she slams the door behind her, 'The Letter' falls in a great bundle of crackling sound under the table. The lights change and the harsh strip-lighting effect transforms the mysterious atmosphere of the room. The Cleaner comes in pushing her cleaning trolley and singing: 'and she flies high like a bird[...]da da tut da da etc. [...]' She starts cleaning and sweeping. In her long handled dust-pan she picks up 'The Letter'*]
Cleaner:	This is a nice bit of stuff. Neither leather nor material, strong though! Perhaps they're chucking it. Well, suppose it's for the bin, shame to waste it. I'll have it. Theodora could use it for her woodwork project, that old guitar case she's been phaffing over all the year. It'd stretch well and good as lining. As for the gobbledygook, well she could say it's modern music, right! Yeah, I think I'll have that. [*She picks up the ancient parchment and carefully folding it into several squares, tucks it into her overalls, and continues with her cleaning duties, singing as she goes*] Look what they done to her song, look what they done to her [....].
	[*As she mops and dusts, all the while singing, the lights go down*]

[*Curtains*]
The End

Partou Zia

Mimesis in Practice

Trish Lyons

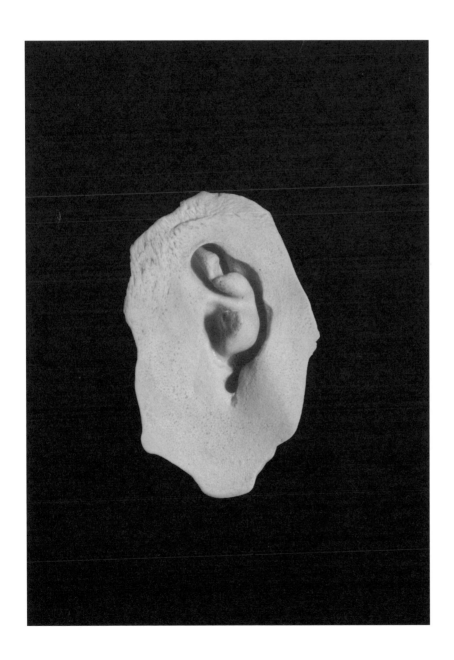

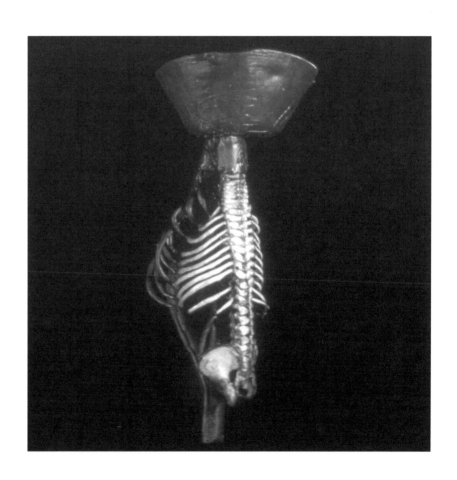

Trish Lyons

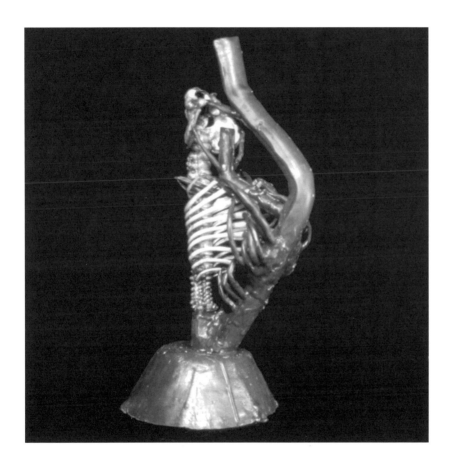

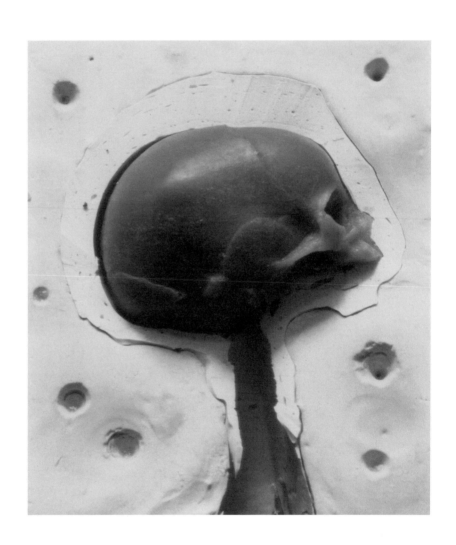

Trish Lyons

mould /məʊld/ *n.& v.* **1** the earth of a grave.
& **2** earth regarded as material of human body, decay
to dust, the dust into which human body 'returns' after
death. & **3** the top or dome of the head, fontanelle in
an infant's head. & **4** hollow form or matrix into which
fluid material is cast so as to form an object of a
particular shape.

Excerpts from *sidekick*[1]

Elizabeth Price

Abstract

sidekick is a descriptive text which annotates the incremental progression of a labout-intensive activity. This activity is fairly straightforward: packing tape is wound from the roll upon which it is commercially distributed, onto itself, to form a sphere. I call this sphere **boulder**.

boulder was started in 1996 and is ongoing. It was initiated with a simple task, yet the repetition of this task incited certain material inevitabilities. As the sphere became larger and its surface area increased, the process became slower because the tape had a gradually decreasing relative impact. Each roll added to the sphere lessened the value of the next and after a while the addition of a roll was impossible to detect. At the present moment of time the ratio of time-spent to visible result is so protracted, that it is difficult to perceive the effects of my action. One of the critical problems of this work, has been knowing how to conclude it – the slippage of the labour out of the range of visible cause and effect, has made it difficult to know how to act. I have resigned myself to continuing it indefinitely.

sidekick was initiated in 1997. It was started when the boulder began to slow down. It is ongoing.

.............I unwind packing tape from the roll upon which it is commercially distributed. As I unwind it from the roll, I rewind it again, but not onto a roll, only onto itself. I wind the entire roll in this way without interruption. At the conclusion of one roll I continue with another, and so on, adding each to the same mass. Gradually the mass grows larger. I maintain this process without any fundamental changes.

I apply the tape to the mass in a consistent and particular manner, and this has allowed the production of a regular form. I wind the tape off the roll and around the mass. In the course of each circuit, I rotate the mass a little, and steer the tape aside, moving it around and across the surface. A circuit does not ever conclude by a return to the precise point at which it started, (although nearly). Because of this the tape is continuously applied to a different area of the surface. The mass expands fairly evenly around an approximately central point of rotation and forms a vague sphere.

The tape is always applied tidily. I draw it tautly over the surface of the sphere, so that it adheres well and lies flat. As I pull the tape across the surface, I smooth it down firmly with the flat of my hand. I apply this pressure at the instance in which the adhesive of the tape makes contact with the surface of the sphere. This keeps the tape open and wide during the application, otherwise the pulling can pucker it along its length, folding it in upon itself, and causing ripples and tucks. I also press out any small air pockets. It is not possible to entirely avoid the occurrence of these quirks, but I am able to minimize them to the degree that they will not physically disrupt or visibly affect the surface of the subsequent layer. On the uppermost layer they can always be seen, but they are slight, and on the whole this top layer is able to cohere as a consistent surface.

Because the tape is always applied with the adhesive on the inside, the 'surface' of the sphere is effectively comprised of the upper-face of the tape (the shiny side). Although, as the sphere is so neatly assembled, and because the tape is such a consistent material, the integrity of the tape does become a little lost to the sphere. It conglomerates, and even at quite close proximity the sphere can seem to have its own surface, which is soft, smooth and glossy. It does not look perfect. It is never

JVAP 2 (1&2) 108–112 ©Intellect Ltd 2002

absolutely spherical. Sometimes, and from some aspects, it can seem to be quite irregularly shaped. Even when it seems nearly round its surface is dimpled all over, and these dimples can vary in their size. The sphere is mid-brown, the same colour as the tape. Although the mass of it and the convex, contoured surface it has produced in that mass, exaggerate and prompt.... It resembles cheap chocolate or all the colours of plasticine together. It looks like a big 'malteser' or a boulder, or an asteroid.

The mass is able to assume some of its own characteristics, but with a close inspection it can always be seen that it is tape. The uppermost strips can be distinguished from the mass of the sphere by means of the edges of the tape which appear as faint lines. The tape is slightly darker at the edge than it is on the face of the tape, because a thread of the adhesive is exposed there, which attracts dust and discolours. Also, however carefully the tape is applied the tiny wrinkles and pleats occur, which tend to delineate the nature of the strip and disclose the process of application. This occurs partly because the tape is flat and the boulder is round and irregular. The present relation of the scale of the tape to the sphere means that the tape is always applied over a convex area, so it cannot be applied completely smoothly. As the sphere gradually increases in scale, I imagine that these conditions of the 'flatness' of the tape will become less significant. At some point the curve of the expanding surface will begin to fall within the scope of the tape's limited flexibility. It will then be possible to apply the tape flat to the surface of the sphere. This development may reduce the visibility of the tape. But although this expansion of the sphere will efface some indications of its material and process, I am not sure of the degree to which it will ever be possible to eradicate all of the inevitable idiosyncrasies of manual application. Even on a flat surface it is difficult to apply the tape evenly: the plastic is light and the glue is strong. The tape is quite a difficult material to manage, and you get only one attempt to apply it. Anyway, obviously the more you try to train and order the application, the more acute the small variables become, manifestly outside the scope of the performed manipulation. And even if these visual indications become very slight, it will still always be possible to verify both the material and the process by the means of touch. You can feel the edges of the tape.

The careful process of application which I employ also has other effects. The tight and precise process of winding results in a dense and highly compacted mass. The sphere is quite heavy, relative to its size. (I have not actually weighed it but I can no longer lift it alone). If I wound it less carefully it would obviously expand more quickly, relative to the time and material expended; although it would probably be a less regular shape and a less stable mass. It includes a large amount of tape, more than I could have speculated in anticipation. I am not sure how many rolls I have wound onto it so far. I lost count around about one hundred, and that was a while ago.
It has also consumed a considerable amount of time. The process of its production is labour intensive and physically demanding. When I began to make it I was keen and curious, and I worked on it for several hours every day. Now I tend to work on it more sporadically, because it does not draw nearer to a point of completion, and no distinct development ever appears to be precipitated. As it grows larger it expands more slowly, so working a little and regularly can appear to make no difference. I tend to work on it intermittently, but then very intensively, in order to be rewarded by some kind of effect. The more I work on it, the more difficult it becomes to work on. It takes more time, relatively, and becomes increasingly physically demanding. It is

now quite unwieldy. It is much too heavy to lift and is quite difficult to manoeuvre because it is too large to encircle with my arms. I have resorted to moving it by rolling it. Although because it is so heavy, rolling tends to compact it. This renders progress even slower.

I do work hard to wind the tape as tightly as possible. Lately I tend use the weight of the thing to aid me, pulling the tape hard against the force of this weight and folding it down quickly onto the surface. This is one respect in which the expansion of the sphere is able to assist in the process. When it was smaller and lighter, I used to produce this stress by pulling between the sphere in one hand and the roll in the other. It was quite difficult to maintain this tension consistently. But even now that it has become a little easier, I can still never wind the tape tightly enough.

It surprises me to observe how much the mass yields under the pressure of its own weight. It is obviously still quite slack, notwithstanding my exertion. Indeed although the sphere is dense and weighty, it is still soft and unstable. Much more so than on the roll. If you apply even slight pressure to a newly applied surface of the sphere, it gives way a little, and bears an impression, like damp clay. However tightly the tape is wound onto the sphere, it is never so taut as on the roll.

As the sphere becomes larger, the gradual accumulation of its weight continues the process of compaction, and increases its relative effect. It is now sufficiently heavy to markedly compress the part of the surface upon which it rests. Whilst I am working on the sphere, it continually rests upon different areas of its surface, and so this compaction is distributed more or less evenly. But if I leave it in one place for a while, then the effect is more evident, and a flat plane develops and slowly expands. Before the mass begins to settle in this way, it also shifts. Occasionally some internal movement of weight upsets the balance and it rolls slightly, without any immediate external cause.

The sphere is quite big now. I get confused about exactly how big it is. Obviously it is always changing in size, but this scarcely happens rapidly. I have not measured it, partly because it is an irregular form, which would be difficult to measure accurately. I usually only need any kind of measurement when the sphere is not on hand to refer to, and in these cases I attempt to rely upon memory. Later on when I am able to actually observe the thing again, I am sure that I guessed wrong. I think that I usually imagine it as bigger than it really is.

But even though I do not know any measurements, the experience of physically working upon it does allow a more immediate awareness of scale. For example, it is too large to go through some doors and it is too heavy for me to lift. It can only be situated in and worked on in places with appropriate access facilities, and lifted with assistance or equipment. On a more refined level, although it is always incrementally changing, at any point it requires a quite precise amount of physical force to roll it, and then to contain and guide this movement. It takes a specific amount of time to roll the thing around full circle, and only a certain length of tape can be pulled from the roll and laid over the accessible surface before it is necessary to pause and roll the sphere over again in order to carry on. I understand these amounts of time and stuff and force quite precisely. I am also able to employ this understanding quite consistently. I can modulate and project this understanding in tandem with the incremental development of the sphere.

Elizabeth Price

I find it more difficult, however, to comprehend the relation of the thing's size, to the quantity of tape used to produce it. In this case immediate practical experience does not really help. In fact even when the sphere is immediately in front of me, and its size is manifest, I am confused about how this discloses quantity.

The roll of tape, however, clearly lends itself well to estimates of quantity. It is a distinct and apparently consistent unit. Large amounts of the material are distributed as multiples of this unit. The rolls are packaged in groups of six, shrinkwrapped together, then stacked into boxes. The roll size must be consistent to allow for this packaging. Each packed box holds six layers or 36 rolls of tape.

Accompanying information indicates that the length of tape upon the roll is 66 metres. With this information I can figure how many metres of tape there are in a box. The tape is five centimetres wide, so I can calculate the square metres of tape included in a roll, and in the box. If I accept or can verify the length and apparent consistency of the roll, then I can deduce quite explicit information about the quantity of tape on a roll, and in a box etc. But although such information is explicit, it is limited and/or selective. It accounts very effectively for certain characteristics of the roll of tape. It describes length and width, which can be extrapolated to produce knowledge of the surface quantity. This understanding is potentially useful, but clearly most apt to the particular moment of application, as the roll is unwound to produce the strip. The information alludes to this strip and the potential length and coverage. The measurements offered by the roll are a promise of the extent of use, and are tailored for those circumstances. But this information is not really readable or testable for the sphere. The information describes a surface for application, and the sphere is clearly a mass. The tape upon the roll could be described in terms of mass, but the only explicit measurement I have, that of the length of tape on a roll, will not help me to deduce this. I would need to know the precise thickness of the tape; the number of revolutions required to wind the roll; the diameter of the cardboard core. It would be quite complicated to calculate the mass from this information. I would find it difficult, and the primary information might be inaccessible anyway.

No information accompanies the tape as it is retailed. At the point of sale only the unit-price is disseminated. The roll does not even include any reference to the quantity it bears. I am aware of the length only because it was detailed in a goods description on an invoice from the manufacturers. (Minimum purchase 100 rolls). I could maybe find out more from this kind of source; but the absence of any kind of information about the tape on the roll is a discouragement. It seems that such information cannot really be important for the tape. The roll does not function to refer to an abstract amount. Its clarity is that of a unit which relies upon familiarity to be understood. It refers only to other rolls, and to cost. And this reference works in general practice, because in common experience tape is not indexed to quantity. It is not exchanged upon a basis of size, weight or length. For it is not conventional to estimate how much tape will be required for a task, and then purchase the appropriate amount accordingly, as with many other consumables. It is not usually bought for a single use, so the actual amount used at one point is probably never considered. It tends to be used over a long period of time, for many small operations, so an entire roll is rarely used without interruption. In fact although the unit of the roll is conventionally accepted as a device for quantifying the tape, in practice it is only considered in relation to cost, in order to judge value for money. The majority of tape manufacturers utilize the same roll size, and include the same amount of tape per roll so this kind of unit comparison is easy to make. Indeed it is so rarely necessary to think of tape in terms of its literal quantity and mass that experience can only allow a very vague appreciation of these things.

So although the unit of the roll is distinct, it is not particularly versatile. It is only ever a rolls-worth and this will not travel. It is not really possible to precisely understand the quantity of tape upon the sphere by exclusive reference to this unit. This sense is lost as the roll is unwound. At the same time it is not possible to properly understand the amount of tape on the sphere by any other means than a reference to the roll, because the roll is the only common concrete unit for the material which exists.

There is a more obvious method of counting, which I have not attempted. So far I have not applied an abstracted system of quantity evaluation to both the sphere and the roll. But this method does bring its own problems and constraints: I can use a measure to verify the exact length of tape upon a roll, but cannot now discover how many rolls have been wound on to the sphere. I did not keep a count, and it cannot be unravelled. I could remove the tape from a single roll, weigh it, weigh the sphere, divide by the first weight and deduce how many rolls of tape it amounted to. I would know how many rolls of tape were incorporated in the sphere, and how heavy, and how long an average roll might be. I would therefore know the length of all of the tape applied to the sphere. I could calculate the average item cost of the roll, and determine the material cost of producing the sphere. This information is more effective via experience of the roll, but it is not a prerequisite. All that is required is the knowledge of the systems used: metres, kilograms, pounds and pence sterling.

The terse economy of these equations is productive. It does reveal, but the same pointed focus which distils common and exchangeable values, is not sensitive enough to register certain crucial contingencies. For example, the information such a calculation produced would be the same for a mass assembled in any way. The mass of tape, of which the sphere is made, infers particular things because of the fact it is wound. It is inflected with the conditions of its production, and implications of time, labour, and action. It seems to me that the issue of the quantity is only really engaging because of its relation to the labour of production. It allows an understanding of the extent of the labour. But the mathematical detail of pure volume, cannot readily be extrapolated to deduce associated issues of duration. In fact it is precisely the material effect of protracted winding which renders it ineffective. For though an understanding of the amount of tape incorporated in the sphere may seem like a way to understand the extent of the labour of its production, any unit of tape cannot be consistently translated into a unit of labour. The quantity of tape upon a roll may remain constant, but the amount of time it takes to apply it to the sphere is not. Overall it incrementally increases with each roll. At some points the increase in scale has rendered progress provisionally quicker, and then slower again, even slower than before; so this development is not even. Also the changes in the nature of the sphere since its inception mean that the character of the labour has similarly evolved. Now it requires quite different kinds of manoeuvres, actions, levels of force, strength and energy than it did at the start.
Such information would require a fairly complicated mathematical sliding scale to estimate and represent it. Obviously this is still possible, although it might prove less articulate, as a illustration of time, labour and stuff than the sphere is itself............

Elizabeth Price